Ultimate Guitar

Chords, Scales & Arpeggios
Handbook

By Damon Ferrante
240 Lessons For All Levels:
Book & Streaming Video Course

Guitar Scales, Chords and Arpeggios
How to Apply Them to Your Music:
How the Book, Streaming Videos, & Audio Files Work

Welcome to this new edition of *The Ultimate Guitar Handbook!* The book, streaming videos and MP3 audio files follow a step-by-step lesson format for learning how to play hundreds guitar scales, chords, licks and arpeggios and how to apply them in the context of your playing. Each lesson builds on the previous one in a clear and easy-to-understand manner to teach you not only how to play the techniques, but also how to use them in your music.

This new edition includes **160 Free Bonus Lessons** and corresponding MP3 audio files that cover guitar licks, scales-over-chords concepts, and chord theory so that you can apply each element in the context your music!

You may download the free bonus lessons (in PDF and MP3 audio format) from the Steeplechase Music Books website:

http://www.steeplechasemusic.com/bonus-lessons.html

This book works as a guide to scales, chords, arpeggios, technique-building exercises, guitar licks, and related music theory. All in all, including the bonus lessons and streaming video lessons, there are over **400 lessons** total!

The scales and arpeggios are written in different keys, so that you will gain proficiency playing along the entire guitar neck. The book provides the most practical fingerings, which will help you learn quickly and play at high velocity. The scales and arpeggios can be played in all keys. As you learn these scale and arpeggio forms, try them in different keys, as well.

At the end of the book, you will be able to play the following scales and arpeggios in every key in 1, 2, and 3 octaves: Major, Minor, Blues Scales, Pentatonic Minor & Major, Modes, Harmonic Minor, Chromatic, Melodic Minor, Whole-Tone, and Octatonic, as well as, Seventh, Diminished, Augmented, Sixth, Ninth, Eleventh, and Thirteenth arpeggios. These are the most useful and common scales for all styles and genres of music.

The Streaming Videos

There are 32 streaming video lessons that correspond to the material presented in the book. The videos are designed to improve your guitar technique, musicality, and give your playing and songwriting more power, color and expressiveness. The videos cover alternate picking techniques, Blues and Rock guitar licks, music theory, legato playing, warm-up exercises, notes on the guitar neck, developing good practice habits and many other guitar techniques.

All of these videos are <u>free</u> and available on <u>Youtube</u> at the <u>Guitar Scales Handbook Channel</u> and the <u>Guitar Arpeggio Handbook Channel</u>. Type "Guitar Scales Handbook" and "Guitar Arpeggio Handbook" into the search field in Youtube. <u>No</u> Registration or Sign-Up is needed to view the steaming videos and there is no limit to the amount of times that they may be viewed.

Table of Contents

Ultimate Guitar Chords, Scales, &
Arpeggios Handbook: 240-Lesson, Step-
By-Step Guitar Guide, Beginner to
Advanced Levels (Book & Videos)

by Damon Ferrante

For additional information about
music books, recordings, and concerts,
please visit the Steeplechase website:
www.steeplechasearts.com

ISBN-13:
978-0615745688 (Steeplechase Arts)

ISBN-10: 0615745687

steepLechase
arts & productions

Steeplechase Music Books

Also by Damon Ferrante

Guitar Adventures: A Fun, Informative, and Step-By-Step 60-Lesson Guide to Chords, Beginner & Intermediate Levels, with Companion Lesson and Play-Along Videos

Piano Scales, Chords & Arpeggios Lessons with Elements of Basic Music Theory: Fun, Step-By-Step Guide for Beginner to Advanced Levels (Book & Videos)

Little Piano Book: Fun, Step-By-Step, Easy-To-Follow, 60-Lesson Song and Beginner Piano Guide to Get You Started (Book & Videos)

Guitar Arpeggio Handbook, 2nd Edition: 120-Lesson, Step-By-Step Guide to Guitar Arpeggios, Music Theory, and Technique-Building Exercises, Beginner to Advanced Levels (Book & Videos)

Guitar Adventures for Kids, Level 1: Fun, Step-By-Step, Beginner Lesson Guide to Get You Started (Book & Videos)

Beginner Piano Elements for Adults: Teach Yourself Piano--Fun, Step-By-Step Beginner to Intermediate Piano Song & Lesson Guide (Book & Videos)

GOOD NEWS!

This edition of *The Ultimate Guitar Handbook* includes free, bonus lessons. Go to the Home Page of SteeplechaseMusic.com. At the top of the Home Page, you will see a link for Guitar Books. Follow the link to the Guitar Books webpage. Then, click on the link for *The Ultimate Guitar Handbook*. Once you are on the webpage for the book, click Bonus Lessons and download the PDF and MP3 Audio Files

Have Fun!

Symbols used in this book

Left-Hand

- **1** · **1st Finger (Index Finger)**
- **2** · **2nd Finger (Middle Finger)**
- **3** · **3rd Finger (Ring Finger)**
- **4** · **4th Finger (Pinky Finger)**
- **(H)** · **Half Step**
- **(W)** · **Whole Step**
- **(W)(H)** · **Whole and Half Steps**

Videos:

- · **There are 32 Streaming videos that correspond to the lessons in this Book.**
- · **The Videos provide background tracks to improvise with the scales.**
- · **These Videos are Free and Available on <u>Youtube</u> at the <u>Guitar Scales Handbook</u> Channel**
- · **No Registration is needed to view the Videos and there is no limit to the amount of times they may be viewed.**

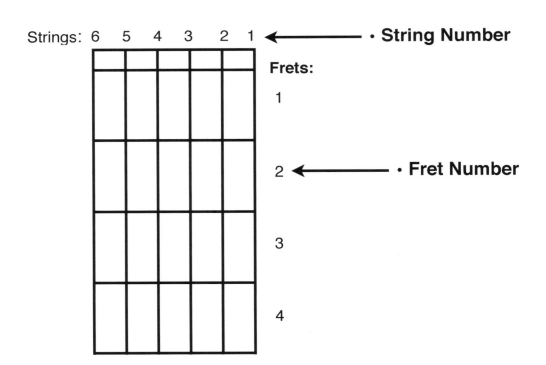

Strings: 6 5 4 3 2 1 ←——————— · **String Number**

Frets:

1

2 ←——————— · **Fret Number**

3

4

Chart 1:
Notes on the 5th & 6th Strings

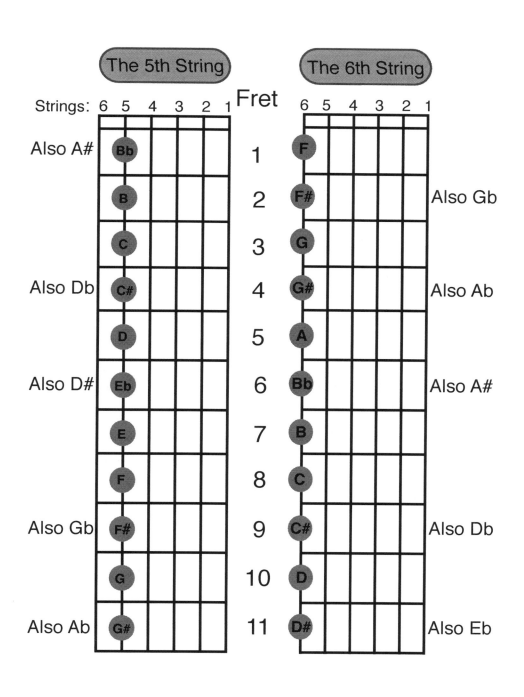

Chart 2:
Notes on the 4th & 3rd Strings

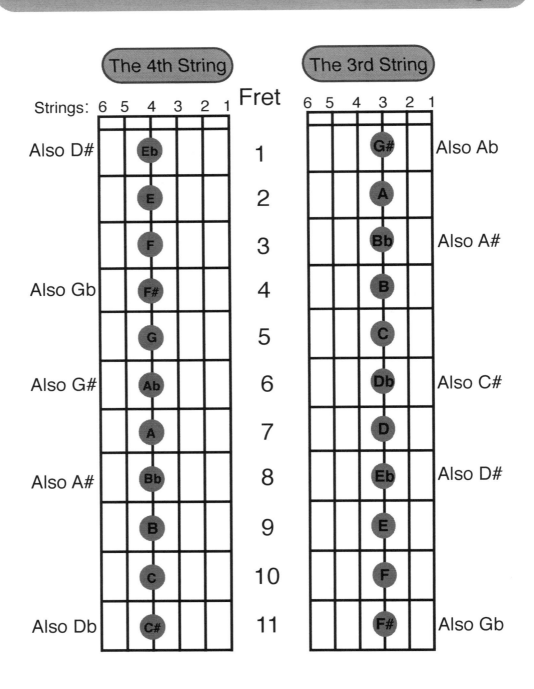

Chart 3:
Notes on the 2nd & 1st Strings

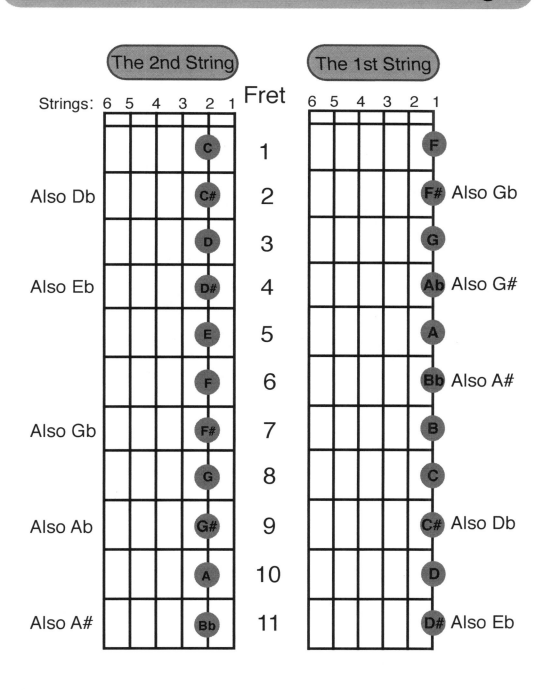

Guitar Scales

Section

1

Pentatonic Minor
Scale & Modes
("Blues Scales")
Starting on the
6th String

Table of Contents for Scales

A Few Words About Scales, Part 1

- Scales are groups of notes that are arranged in stepwise patterns, either going up or down.

- Half Steps and Whole Steps are the most common Steps (distances) between notes of a scale.

- A Half Step is the distance between two frets. For example, from fret 1 to fret 2 on the 6th String (Low E String) is a Half Step: the notes F to F#. Take a look at Chart 1 (on the previous page) and find these notes on the 6th String.

- A Whole Step is the distance between three frets. For example, from fret 1 to fret 3 on the 6th String (Low E String) is a Whole Step: the notes F to G. Take a look at Chart 1 (on the previous page) and find these notes on the 6th String.

- The combinations of Half Steps and Whole Steps create the particular character for each scale. For example, a Major Scale sounds different than a Minor Scale, because there is a different arrangement of Half Steps and Whole Steps in each scale.

- In this book, the scales are grouped based on type and arranged by the level of technique required to play them: from beginner to advanced.

A Few Words About Scales, Part 2

- The Scales in this book follow 2 basic fingering patterns: Scales that begin on the 6th String and Scales that begin on the 5th String. See Chart 1 for the notes of the 5th and 6th Strings.

- All of the Scales in this book can be played in every key. For example, the pattern for the G Major Scale, found in Lesson 24, can be transposed ("moved") to any other key by moving the pattern to another position on the guitar neck.

- All of the Scales in this book follow a 2-Note-Per-String or 3-Note-Per-String Pattern. These are the easiest and most practical Scale Patterns to learn. They will allow you to learn many of the scales in this book quickly, since they all follow the same basic finger patterns.

- When learning a new scale, first, learn the finger pattern on one string. Then, add a second-string finger pattern and practice these patterns together. Gradually, add additional strings.

- Along with the scale patterns, there are music theory sections.

- There are also free Play-Along Video Jam Tracks. So, you can try improvising with the scales.

*Check out the video lesson on basic technique.

Lesson 1: Pentatonic Minor: Introduction & Modes

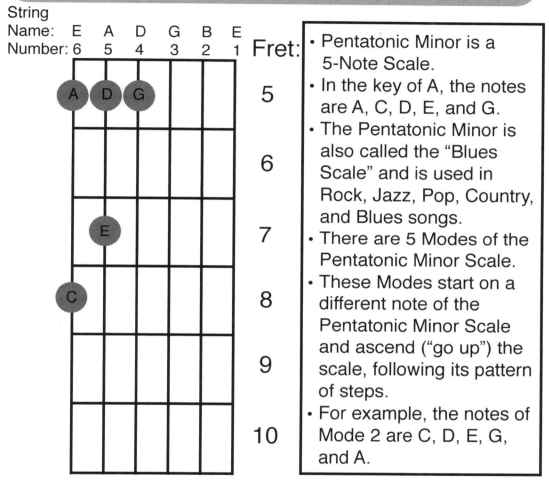

String Name: E A D G B E
Number: 6 5 4 3 2 1
Fret:
5
6
7
8
9
10

- Pentatonic Minor is a 5-Note Scale.
- In the key of A, the notes are A, C, D, E, and G.
- The Pentatonic Minor is also called the "Blues Scale" and is used in Rock, Jazz, Pop, Country, and Blues songs.
- There are 5 Modes of the Pentatonic Minor Scale.
- These Modes start on a different note of the Pentatonic Minor Scale and ascend ("go up") the scale, following its pattern of steps.
- For example, the notes of Mode 2 are C, D, E, G, and A.

A Pentatonic Minor Notes

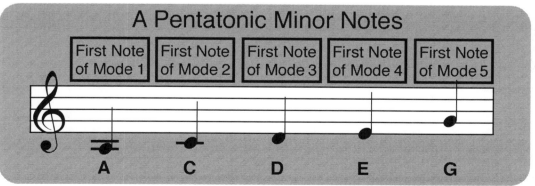

First Note of Mode 1	First Note of Mode 2	First Note of Mode 3	First Note of Mode 4	First Note of Mode 5
A	C	D	E	G

*Check out the video lesson on Blues Guitar, Part 1.

Lesson 2: A Pentatonic Minor: Mode 1: 6th String, 5th Fret

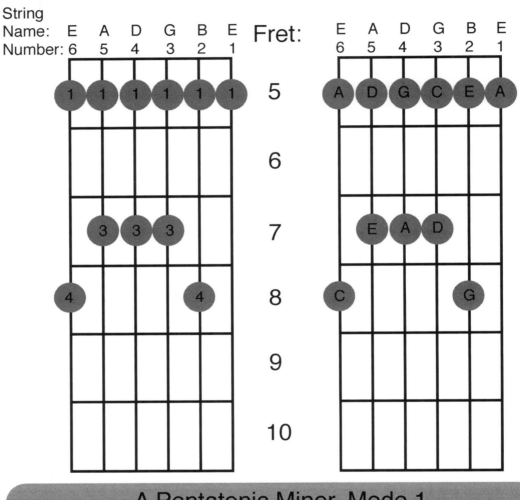

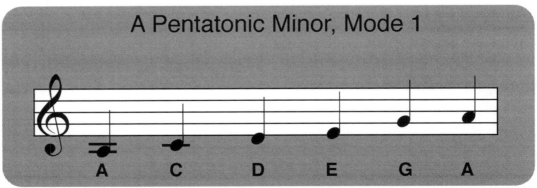

A Pentatonic Minor, Mode 1

Technique Interlude: Alternate Picking

Here are two alternate-picking exercises (in tablature / TAB format) to improve your right-hand picking technique. Repeat each exercise at a comfortable tempo for between 1 and 2 minutes. If your hands start to feel tired, just shake them out and take a break for a while.

⊓ : This symbol stands for a downstroke.

∨ : This symbol stands for an upstroke.

```
   ⊓  ∨  ⊓  ∨  ⊓  ∨  ⊓  ∨
───0──1──0──1──0──1──0──1────  High-E String
─────────────────────────────  B String
─────────────────────────────  G String
─────────────────────────────  D String
─────────────────────────────  A String
─────────────────────────────  Low-E String


   ⊓  ∨  ⊓  ∨  ⊓  ∨  ⊓  ∨
───1──2──1──2──1──2──1──2────  High-E String
─────────────────────────────  B String
─────────────────────────────  G String
─────────────────────────────  D String
─────────────────────────────  A String
─────────────────────────────  Low-E String
```

*Check out the video lesson on alternate picking.

Lesson 3: A Pentatonic Minor: Mode 2: 6th String, 8th Fret

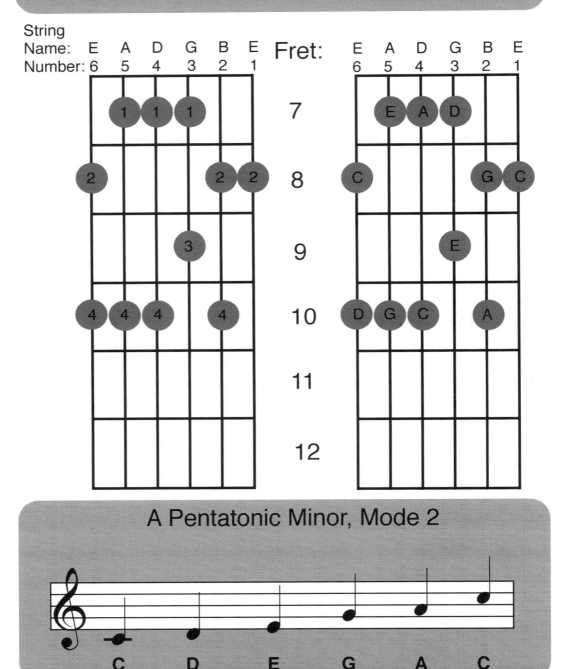

A Pentatonic Minor, Mode 2

C   D   E   G   A   C

Lesson 4: A Pentatonic Minor: Mode 3: 6th String, 10th Fret

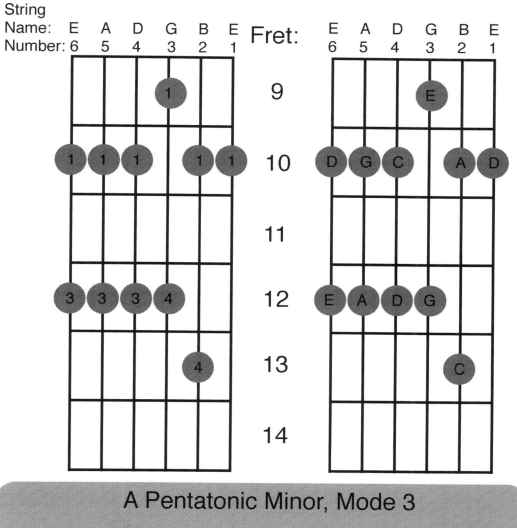

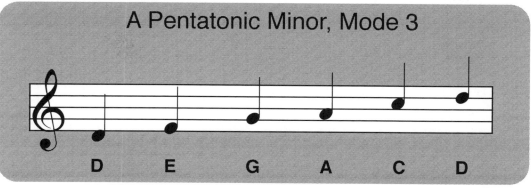

A Pentatonic Minor, Mode 3

D E G A C D

Lesson 5: A Pentatonic Minor: Mode 4: 6th String, 12th Fret

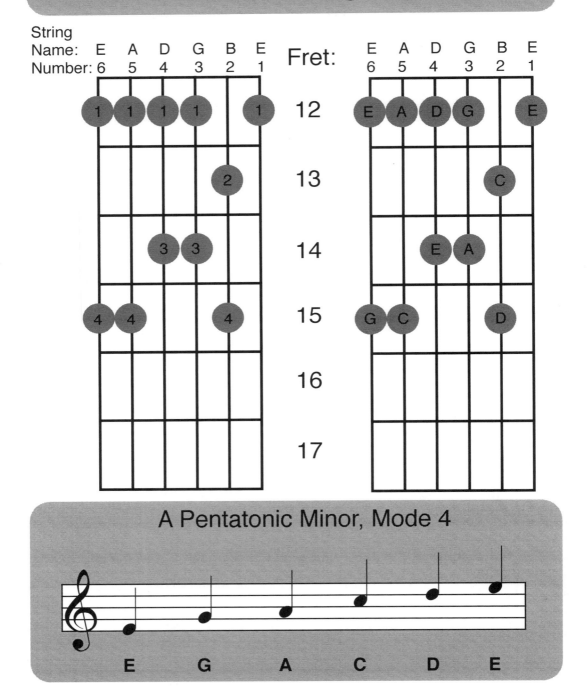

A Pentatonic Minor, Mode 4

E G A C D E

Lesson 6: A Pentatonic Minor: Mode 5: 6th String, 15th Fret

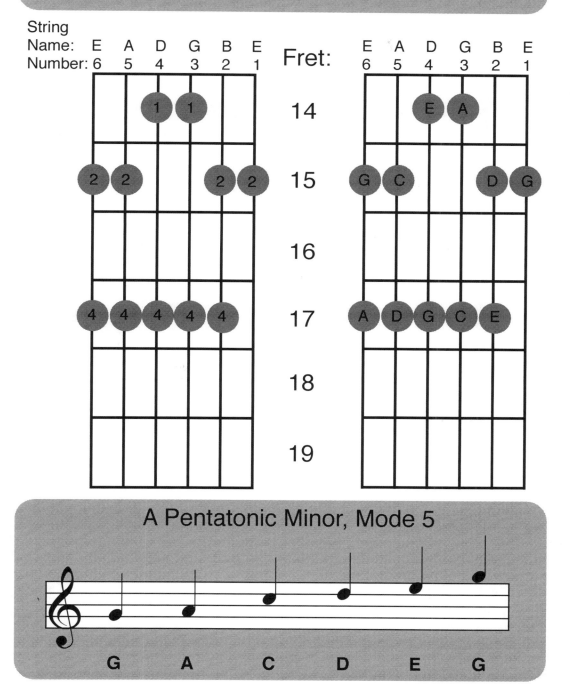

A Pentatonic Minor, Mode 5

G A C D E G

Lesson 7: A Pentatonic Minor: Mode 1: 6th String, 17th Fret

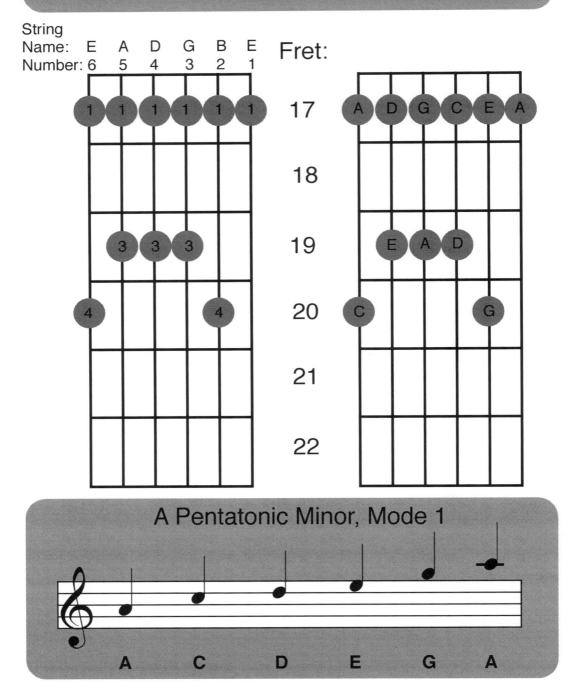

String Name: E A D G B E
Number: 6 5 4 3 2 1

Fret:

17 18 19 20 21 22

A Pentatonic Minor, Mode 1

A C D E G A

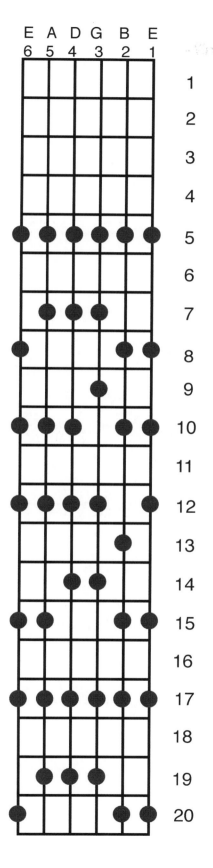

E A D G B E
6 5 4 3 2 1

1
2
3
4
5
6
7
8
9
10
11
12
13
14
15
16
17
18
19
20

Lesson 8: A Pentatonic Minor Notes on the Entire Guitar Neck

• The Chart on the left shows all of the notes of the A Pentatonic Minor Scale that we have learned in this section of the book.

• Take some time studying this chart and naming its notes on the neck. After you name a note, place your finger on the fret for that note. Repeat this process several times over the course of a few days or a week or two. This exercise will begin to greatly improve your understanding of the fretboard. Working on this particular lesson will help demystify some of the note relationships on the fretboard.

• Take your time and have fun!

*Check out the video lesson on Blues Guitar, Part 2.

Lesson 9: Rockabilly
Video 1

Jam Track 1: Rockabilly

$\frac{4}{4}$ A7	A7	A7	A7
D7	D7	A7	A7
E7	D7	A7	A7

- Check out the *Rockabilly* Jam Track on the *Guitar Scales Handbook* Youtube Channel.

- Type "GuitarScalesHandbook" (one word) into the Youtube search bar.

- You can improvise with the A Pentatonic Minor Scale forms from that you have learned in the previous lessons.

Section

2

Major Scale
& Modes
Starting on the
5th String

Lesson 10: Overview: The Major Scale

- All Major Scales Follow the Same Pattern.

- Major Scales Are Composed of a Set Pattern of Half and Whole Steps.

- A Half Step is the Distance from One Fret to the Next Fret on the Guitar. For Example, from Fret 1 to Fret 2 (on any string) is the Distance of a Half Step.

- A Whole Step is made up of 2 Half Steps and is Twice the Distance of a Half Step. For Example, from Fret 1 to Fret 3 (on any string) is the Distance of a Whole Step.

- Whole Steps are indicated with a circled "W".

- Half Steps are indicated with a circled "H".

- Throughout the *Guitar Scales Handbook,* Half Steps and Whole Steps are indicated with these symbols.

C Major Scale with Half Steps and Whole Steps

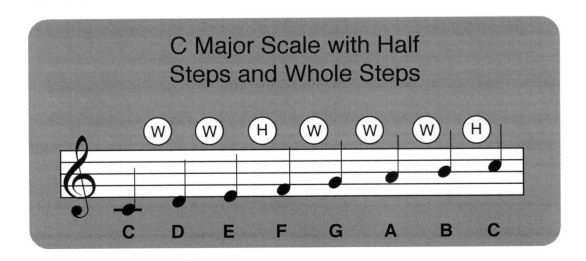

Lesson 11: Overview, Part 1: The Major Scale & Its Modes

- There are 7 Modes of the Major Scale.

- Each Mode begins on one of the notes of the Major Scale.

- The Modes have names that come from Ancient Greek States.

- All Major Scales (in every key) follow this pattern for the Modes.

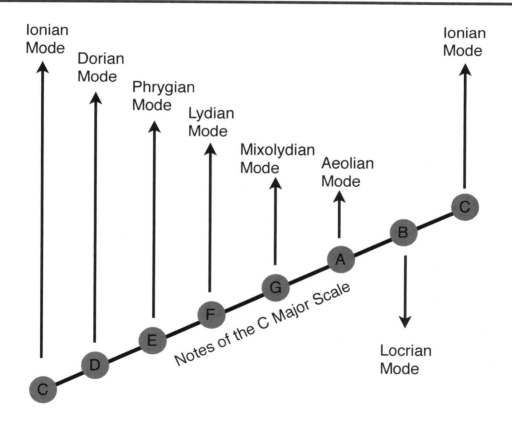

*Check out the video lesson on the major scale.

Lesson 12: Overview, Part 2: The Major Scale & Its Modes

These are the First 4 Modes of the C Major Scale. As you can see, they are built on the notes of the C Major Scale.

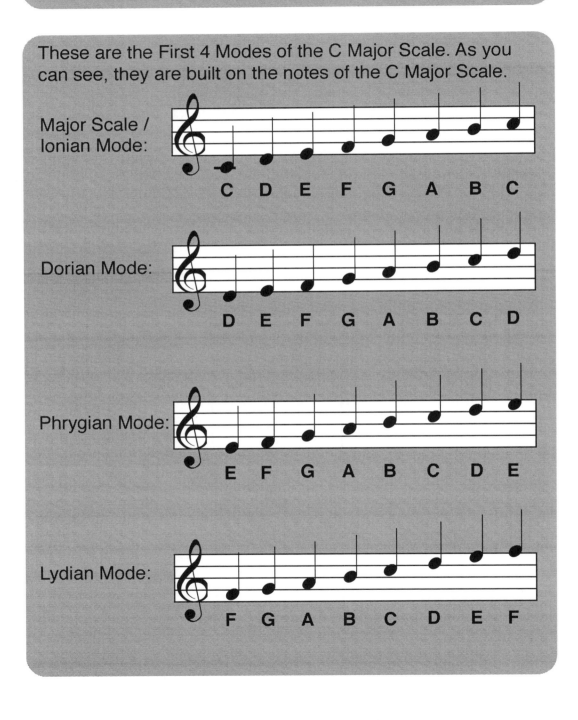

Major Scale / Ionian Mode: C D E F G A B C

Dorian Mode: D E F G A B C D

Phrygian Mode: E F G A B C D E

Lydian Mode: F G A B C D E F

Lesson 13: Major Scale: C Major: 5th String, 3rd Fret

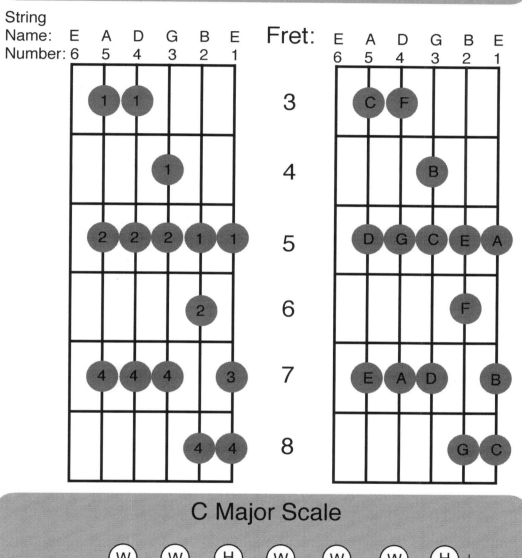

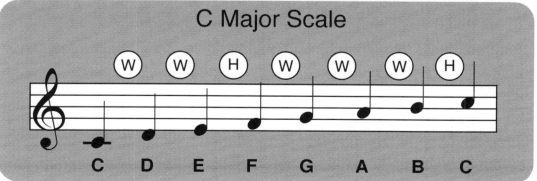

C Major Scale

Lesson 14: Dorian Mode: D Dorian: 5th String, 5th Fret

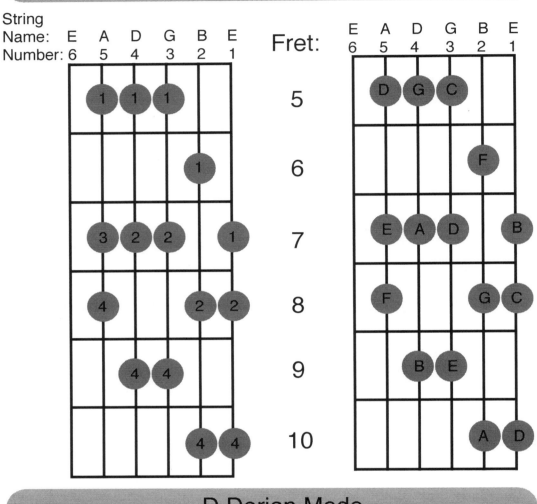

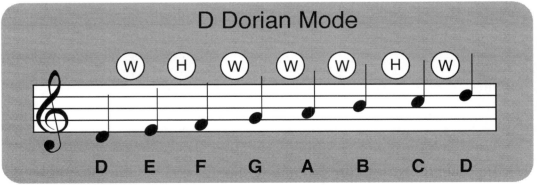

D Dorian Mode

Lesson 15: Phrygian Mode: E Phrygian: 5th String, 7th Fret

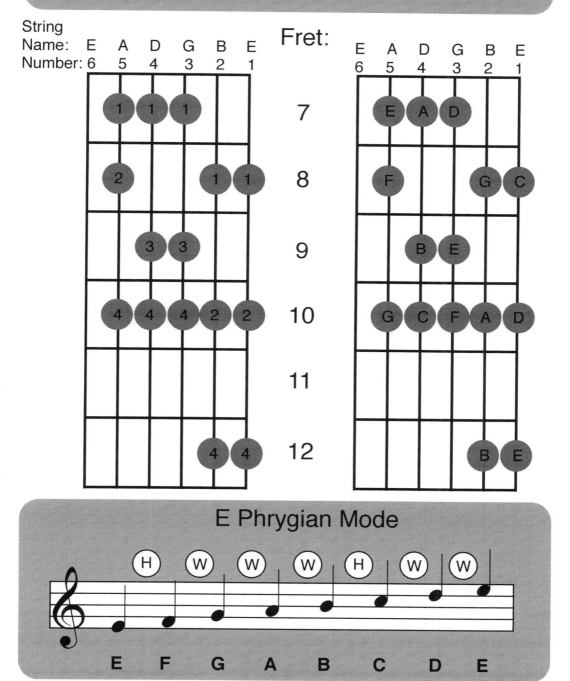

String Name: E A D G B E
Number: 6 5 4 3 2 1

Fret:

E A D G B E
6 5 4 3 2 1

E Phrygian Mode

Lesson 16: Lydian Mode: F Lydian: 5th String, 8th Fret

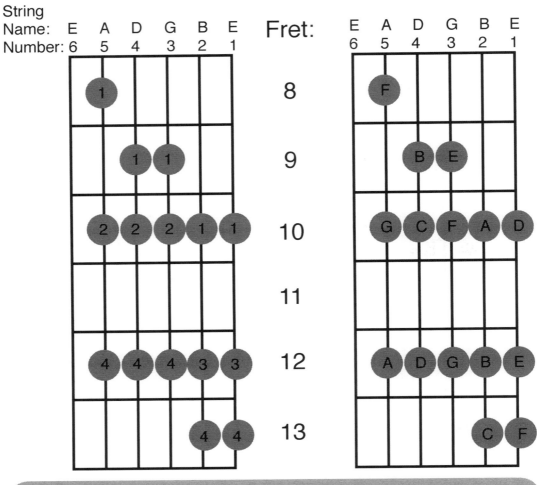

String
Name: E A D G B E Fret: E A D G B E
Number: 6 5 4 3 2 1   6 5 4 3 2 1

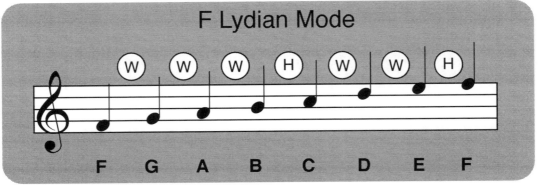

F Lydian Mode

F G A B C D E F

Lesson 17: Overview, Part 3
The Major Scale & Its Modes

- The last 3 Modes of the Major Scale are the Mixolydian, Aeolian, and Locrian.

- They are built on the 5th, 6th, and 7th Notes (also called "Degrees") of the Major Scale.

- The Aeolian Mode is also the Minor Scale.

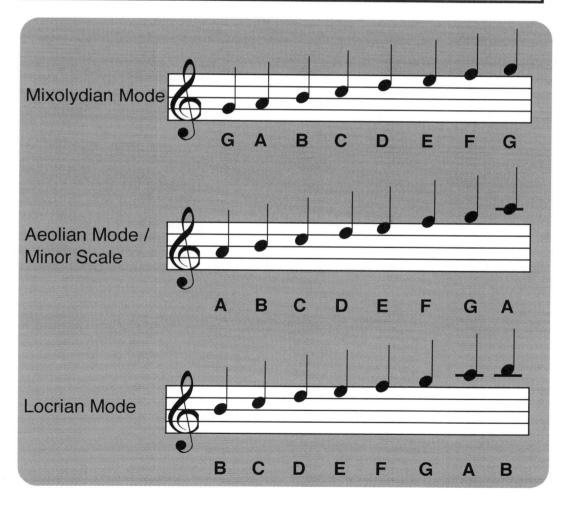

*Check out the video lesson on the minor scale.

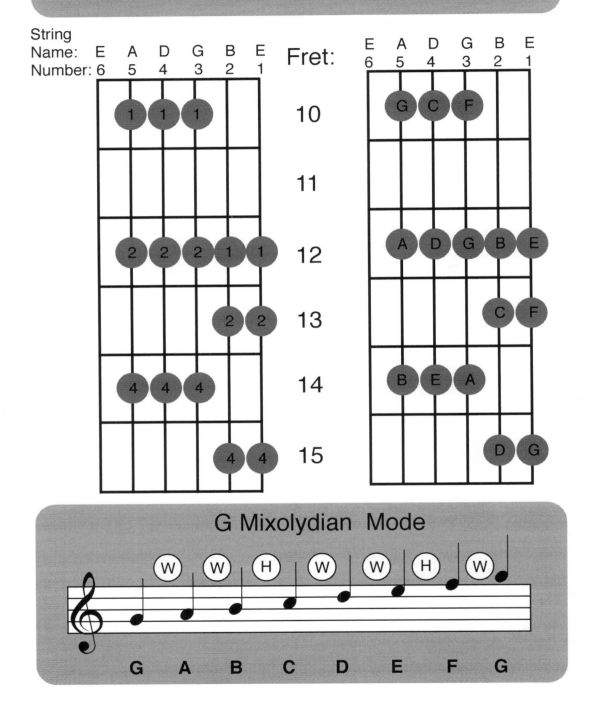

Lesson 19: Minor Scale / Aeolian Mode: A Aeolian: 5th String, 12th Fret

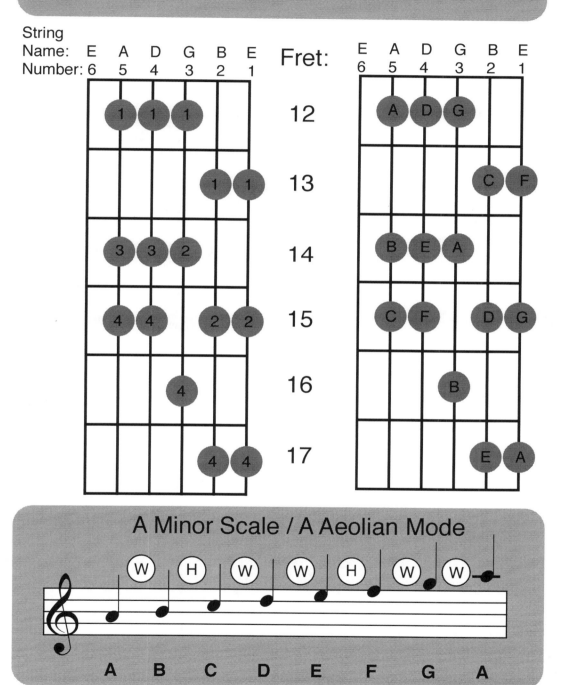

Lesson 20: Locrian Mode: B Locrian: 5th String, 14th Fret

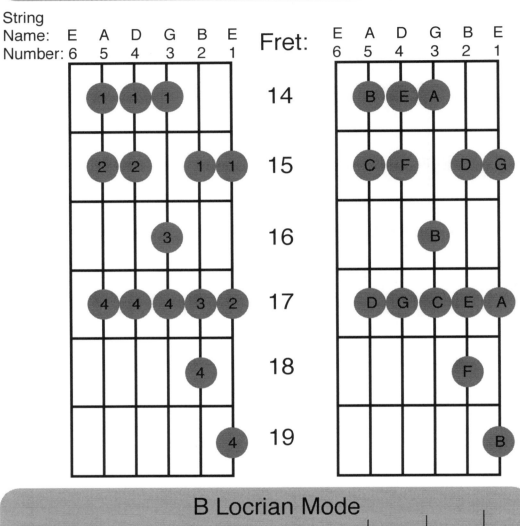

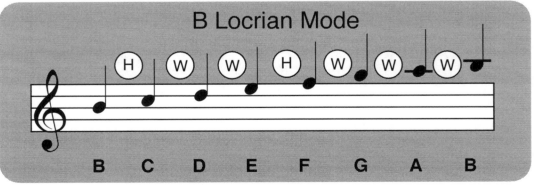

B Locrian Mode

B   C   D   E   F   G   A   B

Lesson 21: Some Ideas on when to use the Lydian, Mixolydian, and Aeolian Modes

- Using the Lydian, Mixolydian, and Aeolian (which is also the Minor Scale) Modes can add variety and greater expressivity to your playing and songwriting.

- The Lydian Mode can be used over Major Chords and Major 7th Chords.

- The Mixolydian Mode works well over Dominant 7th Chords.

- The Aeolian Mode (Minor Scale) sounds good over Minor Chords and Minor 7th Chords.

- In Jam Track 2, try playing the A Lydian, then A Mixolydian, and then the A Aeolian over the Video Track.

- Use the Finger Patterns that you have learned in the last few pages.

- For each of the Scales, Start the Finger Pattern on the <u>12th</u> Fret of the <u>5th</u> <u>String</u>.

- You can find the Video on the GuitarScalesHandbook (all one word) Youtube Channel. ***Have Fun!***

Jam Track 2: Rock Progression in A

$\frac{4}{4}$ | A5 | A5 | E5 | E5 |

Lesson 22: Major Scale: C Major: 5th String, 15th Fret

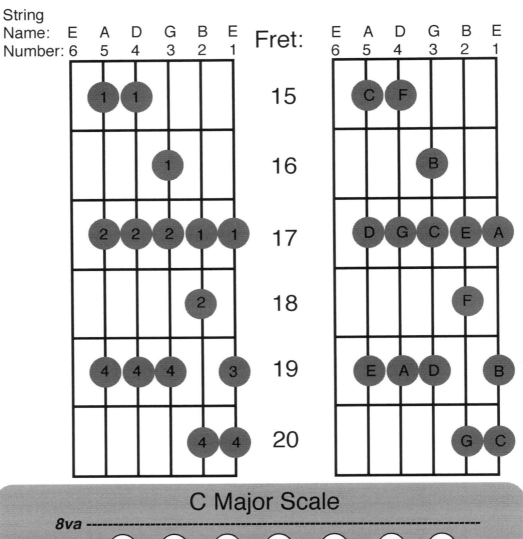

C Major Scale

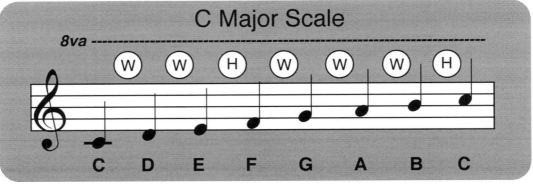

C D E F G A B C

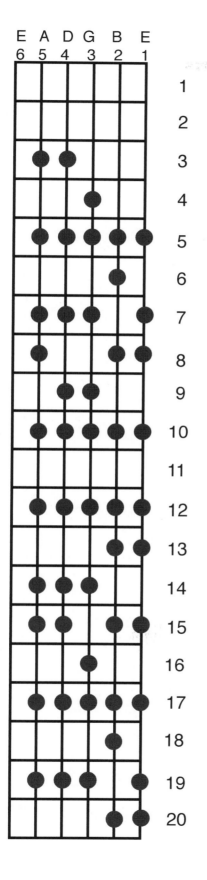

E A D G B E
6 5 4 3 2 1

1
2
3
4
5
6
7
8
9
10
11
12
13
14
15
16
17
18
19
20

Lesson 23: C Major Scale Notes on the Entire Guitar Neck

• The Chart on the left shows all of the notes of the C Major Scale and Modes that we have learned in this section of the book.

• Take some time studying this chart and naming its notes on the neck. After you name a note, place your finger on the fret for that note. Repeat this process several times over the course of a few days or a week or two.

• Once you have become proficient with naming one note, try naming two at a time.

• Try naming two notes at a time on different strings.

• **Check Out Jam Track Video 3!**

Section

3

Major Scale & Modes Starting on the 6th String

Lesson 24: Major Scale: G Major: 6th String, 3rd Fret

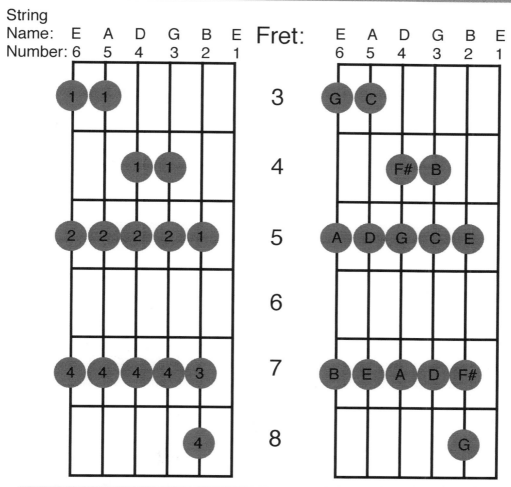

String Name: E A D G B E   Fret: E A D G B E
Number: 6 5 4 3 2 1   6 5 4 3 2 1

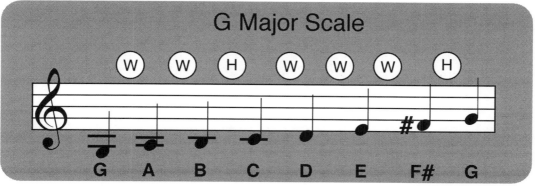

G Major Scale

W W H W W W H

G A B C D E F# G

Lesson 25: Dorian Mode: A Dorian: 6th String, 5th Fret

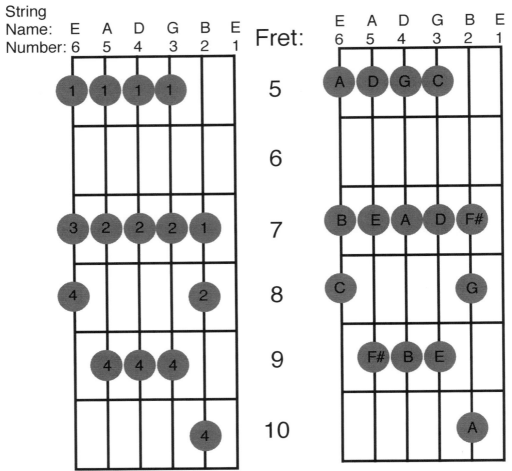

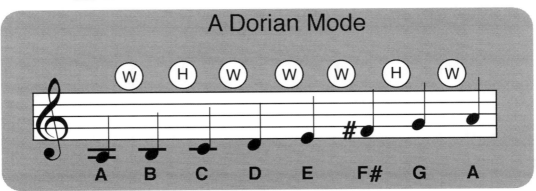

A Dorian Mode

Lesson 26: Phrygian Mode: B Phrygian: 6th String, 7th Fret

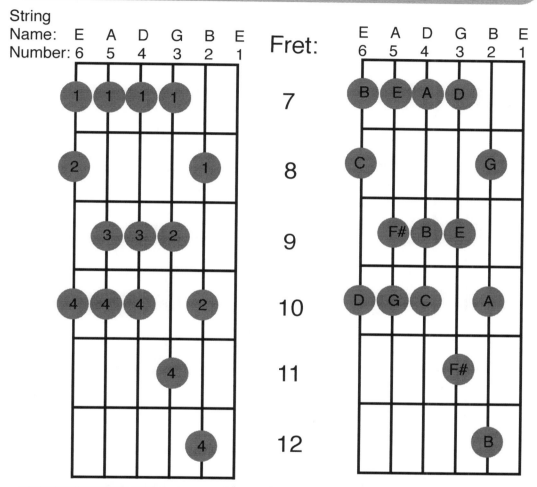

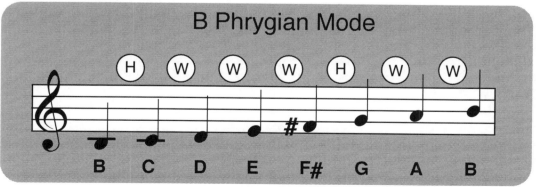

B Phrygian Mode

Lesson 27: Lydian Mode: C Lydian: 6th String, 8th Fret

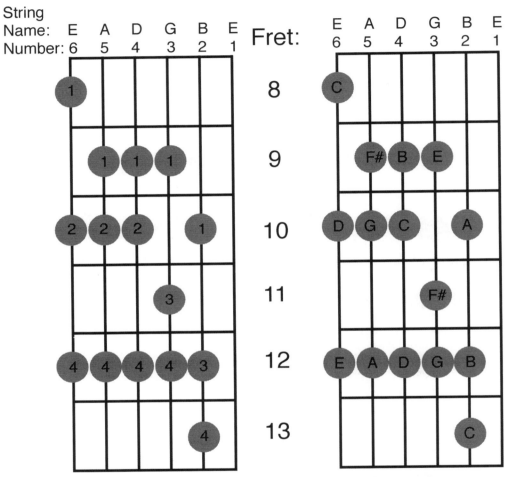

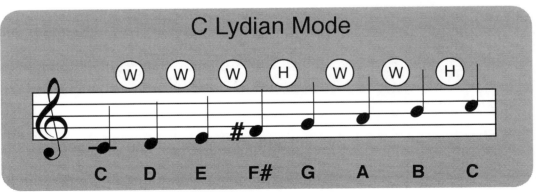

C Lydian Mode

C D E F# G A B C

Lesson 28: Mixolydian Mode: D Mixolydian: 6th String, 10th Fret

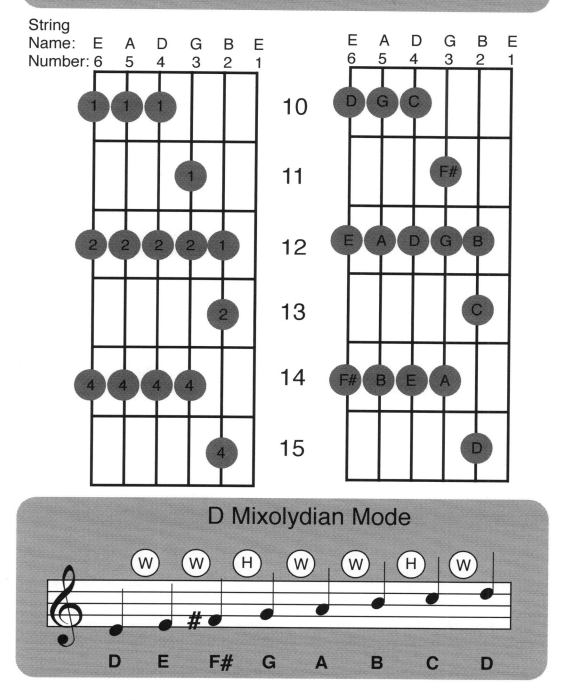

*Check out the video lesson on intervals.

Lesson 29: Minor Scale / Aeolian Mode: E Minor Scale / E Aeolian Mode: 6th String, 12th Fret

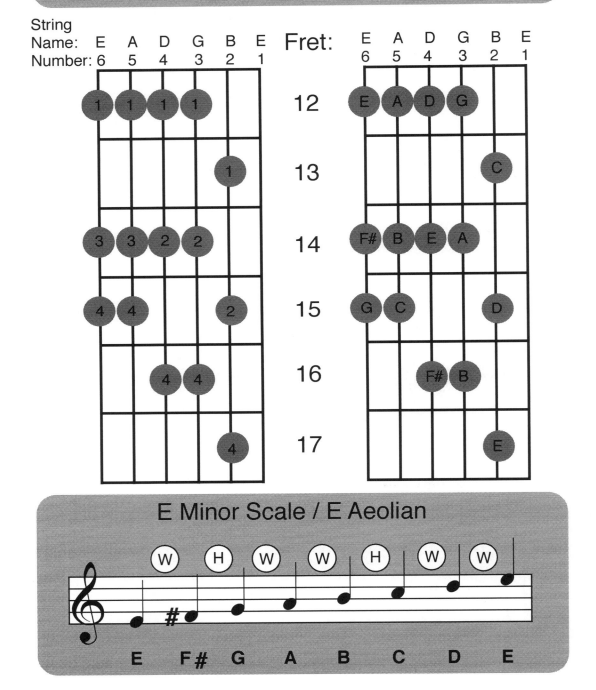

E Minor Scale / E Aeolian

Lesson 30: Locrian Mode: F# Locrian: 6th String, 14th Fret

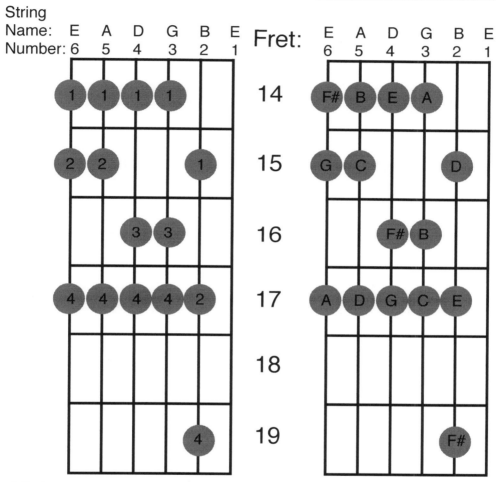

String Name:	E	A	D	G	B	E	Fret:	E	A	D	G	B	E
Number:	6	5	4	3	2	1		6	5	4	3	2	1

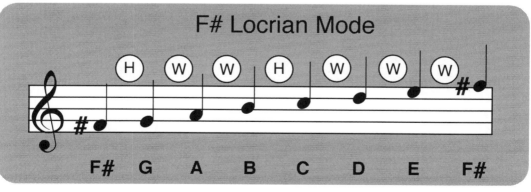

F# Locrian Mode

F# G A B C D E F#

Lesson 31: Major Scale: G Major: 6th String, 15th Fret

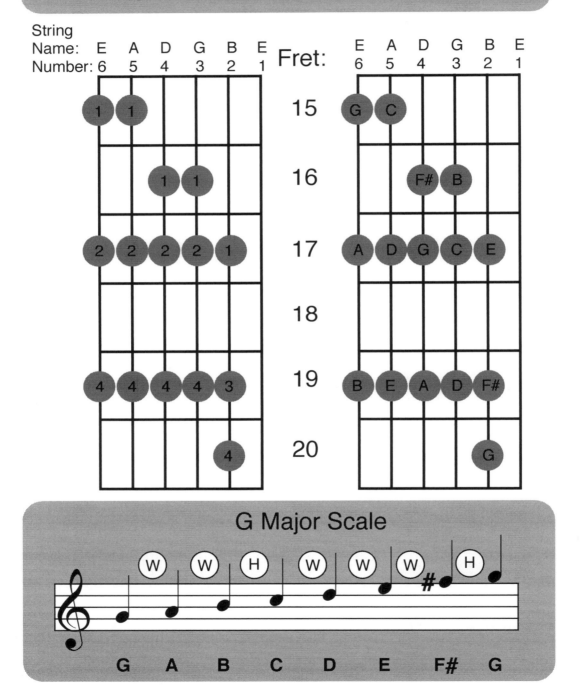

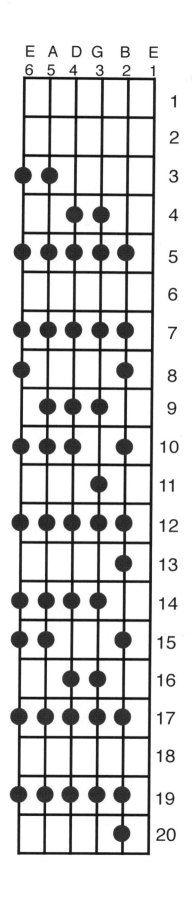

E A D G B E
6 5 4 3 2 1

Lesson 32:
G Major Scale
Notes on the
Entire Guitar Neck

- The Chart on the left shows all of the notes of the G Major Scale Modes Scale that we have looked at in this section of the book.

- Take some time studying this chart and naming its notes on the neck. After you name a note, place your finger on the fret for that note. Repeat this process several times over the course of a few days or a week or two.

- Try naming 3 consecutive notes of a mode and locate them on the chart.

- **Check Out Jam Track Video 4. It is in E Minor. Use the scale pattern from Lesson 29 (12th Fret of the 6th String).**

Section

4

Pentatonic Minor
Scale & Modes
("Blues Scales")
Starting on the
5th String

Lesson 33: D Pentatonic Minor: Mode 1: 5th String, 5th Fret

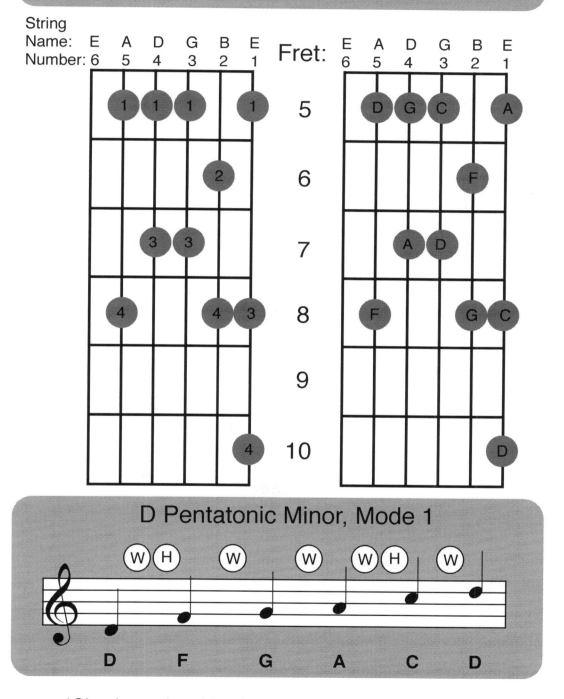

*Check out the video lesson on legato technique.

Lesson 34: D Pentatonic Minor: Mode 2: 5th String, 8th Fret

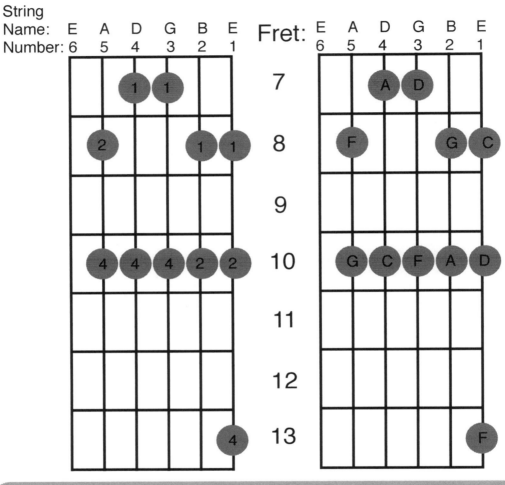

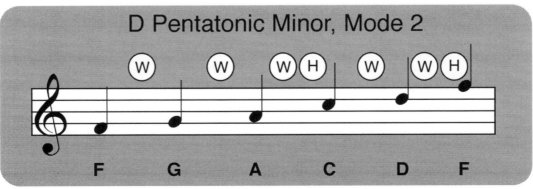

D Pentatonic Minor, Mode 2

F G A C D F

Lesson 35: D Pentatonic Minor: Mode 3: 5th String, 10th Fret

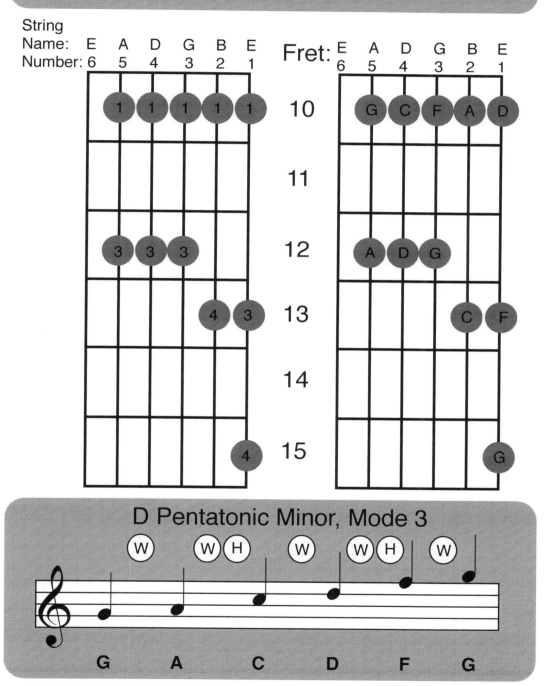

D Pentatonic Minor, Mode 3

Lesson 36: D Pentatonic Minor: Mode 4: 5th String, 12th Fret

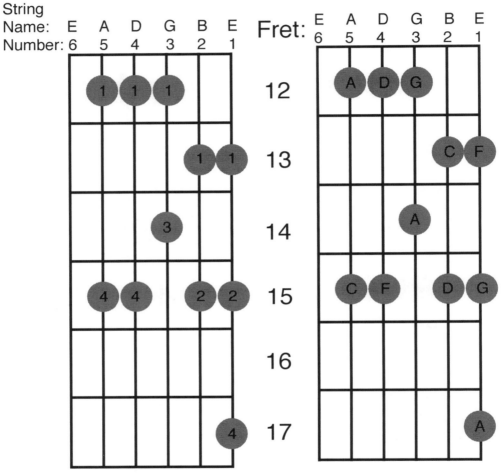

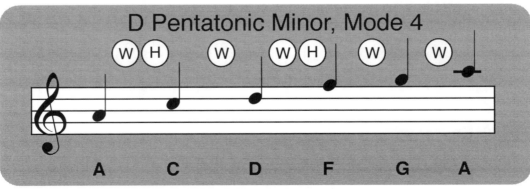

D Pentatonic Minor, Mode 4

A C D F G A

Lesson 37: D Pentatonic Minor: Mode 5: 5th String, 15th Fret

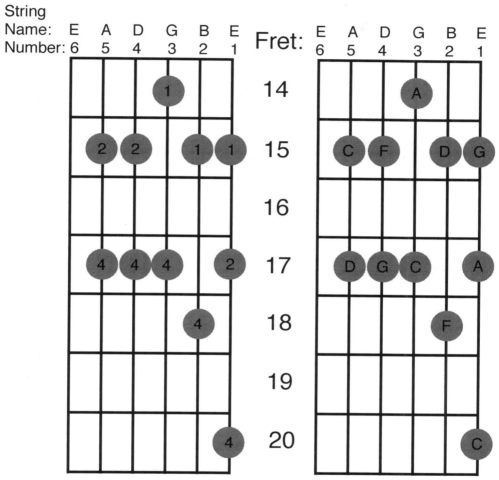

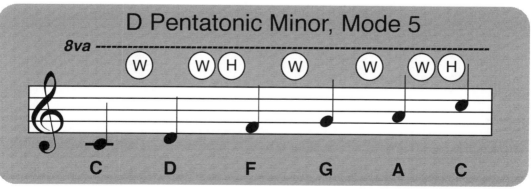

D Pentatonic Minor, Mode 5

Lesson 38: D Pentatonic Minor: Mode 1: 5th String, 17th Fret

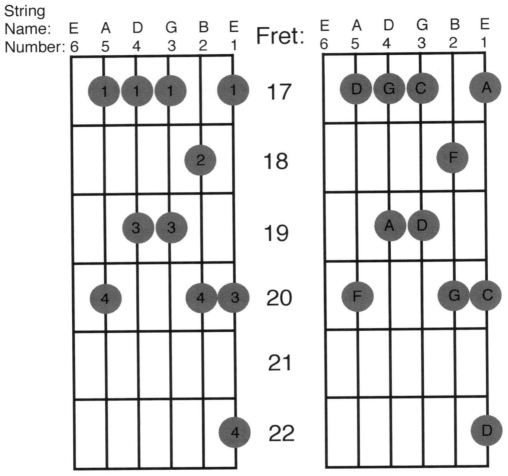

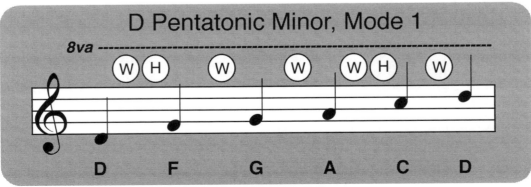

D Pentatonic Minor, Mode 1

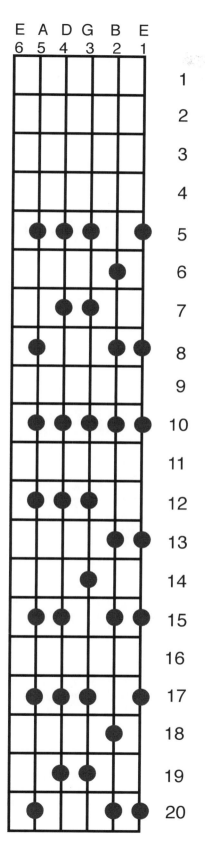

E A D G B E
6 5 4 3 2 1

1
2
3
4
5
6
7
8
9
10
11
12
13
14
15
16
17
18
19
20

- The Chart on the left shows the notes of the D Pentatonic Minor Scale that we have learned in this section of the book.

- Take some time studying this chart and naming its notes on the neck. After you name a note, place your finger on the fret for that note. Repeat this process several times over the course of a few days or a week or two.

- Name 5 consecutive scale notes and find them in different locations on the neck.

- **Check Out Jam Track Video 5: Blues in D!**

Section

5

Natural, Harmonic, & Melodic Minor Scales Starting on the 6th String

Lesson 40: Minor Scale: Overview, Part 1

- Major and Minor Scales have a difference in the character of their sounds.
- Major Scales have a "Brighter" sound. Minor Scales have a "Darker" sound.
- This difference in sound character is created by the arrangement of Half Steps in the Minor Scale.
- In a Minor Scale, there is a Half Step between the 2nd & 3rd Scale Degrees and there is a Half Step between the 5th & 6th Scale Degrees.
- In the Minor Scale, the 7th Scale Degree is also a Half Step Lower.

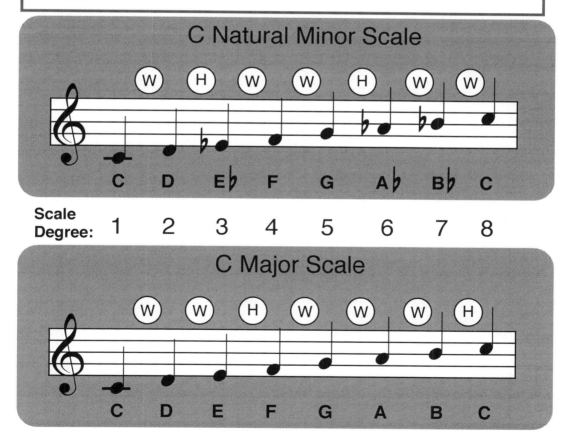

Lesson 41: Minor Scale: Overview, Part 2

- There are two other common forms of the Minor Scale: the Harmonic Minor and Melodic Minor Scales.
- The Harmonic Minor Scale is just like the Natural Minor Scale (a "fancy" name for the Minor Scale), except that between Scale Degrees 6 and 7 there is both a Whole and Half Step. There is also a Half Step between Scale Degrees 7 and 8.
- The Melodic Minor Scale (ascending) is just like the Natural Minor Scale, except that between Scale Degrees 4-8 it is the same as the Major Scale.
- Descending, the Melodic Minor Scale is the same as the Minor Scale.

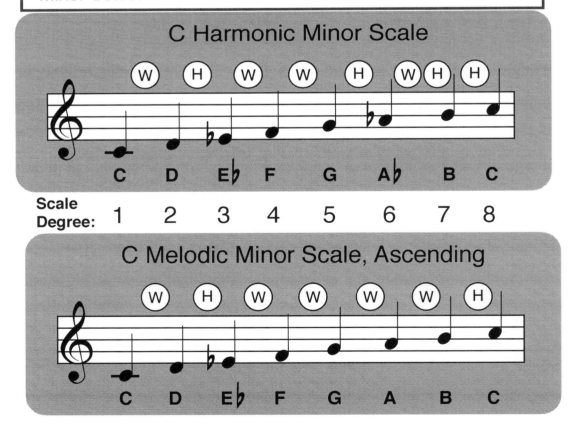

C Harmonic Minor Scale

| W | H | W | W | H | W H | H |

C D E♭ F G A♭ B C

Scale Degree: 1 2 3 4 5 6 7 8

C Melodic Minor Scale, Ascending

| W | H | W | W | W | W | H |

C D E♭ F G A B C

Lesson 42: C Natural Minor: 6th String, 8th Fret

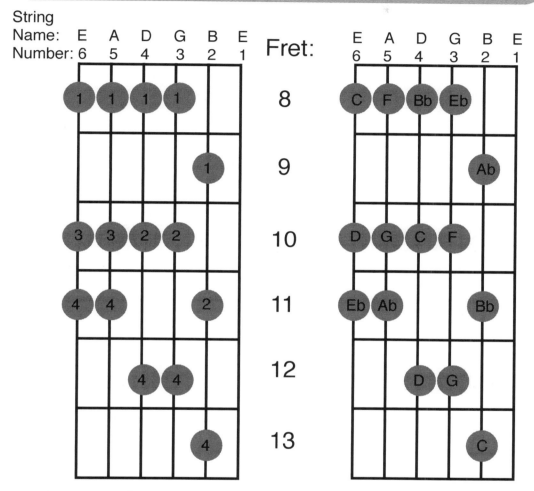

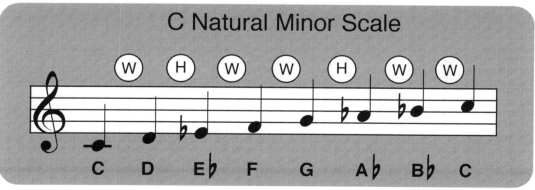

C Natural Minor Scale

Lesson 43: C Harmonic Minor: 6th String, 8th Fret

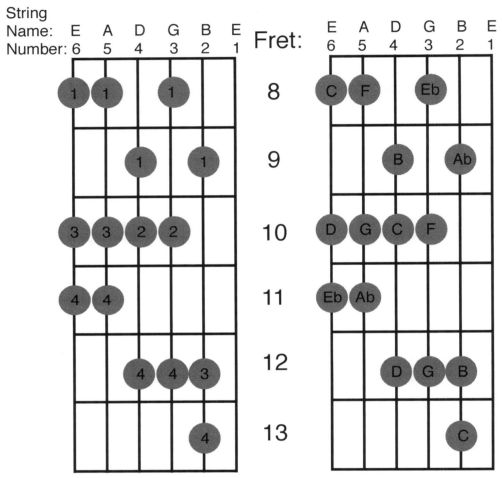

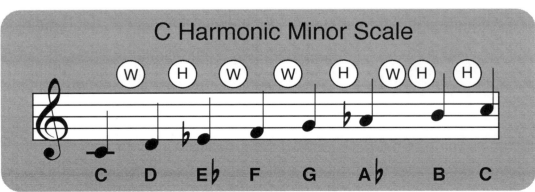

C Harmonic Minor Scale

Lesson 44: C Melodic Minor: Ascending: 6th String, 8th Fret

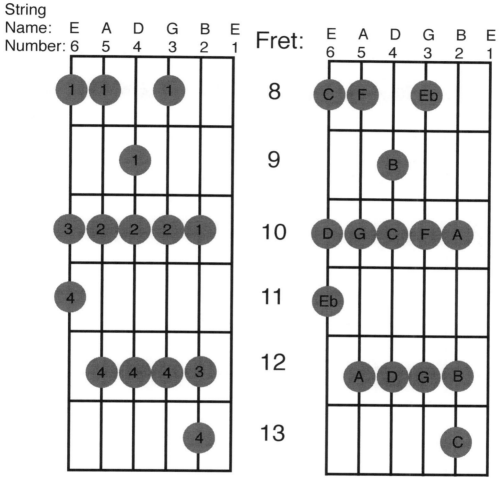

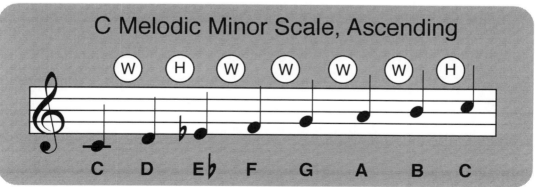

C Melodic Minor Scale, Ascending

Lesson 45: C Melodic Minor: Descending: 6th String, 8th Fret

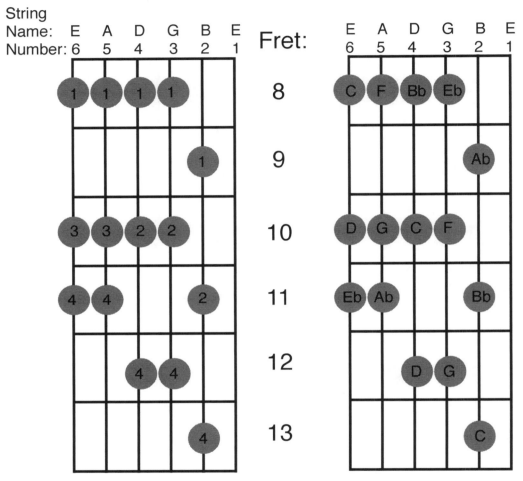

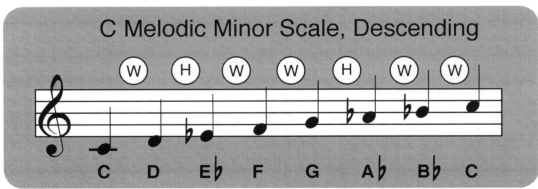

C Melodic Minor Scale, Descending

Lesson 46: Harmonic Minor: An Overview + Jam Track 6

- There is a Half Step between the 7th and 8th Scale Degrees for the Harmonic Minor.

- This gives the Harmonic Minor an exotic character and intensifies the movement from the 7th to the 8th Degree of the scale. For example, in C Harmonic Minor, this is a movement from the note B to C.

- Another characteristic of the Harmonic Minor Scale is that chords built on the 5th Degree of the scale are Major Chords, rather than Minor Chords (like in the Natural Minor Scale).

- In Jam Track 6, try playing the C Harmonic Minor over the Video Track.

- Use the Finger Pattern that you have learned in the last few pages.

- Listen to the exotic quality of the scale.

- You can find the Video on the GuitarScalesHandbook (all one word) Youtube Channel.

Jam Track 6: Harmonic Minor Progression in C

$\frac{4}{4}$ Cm | Cm | G7 | Cm

Section

6

Natural, Harmonic, & Melodic Minor Scales Starting on the 5th String

Lesson 47: E Natural Minor: 5th String, 7th Fret

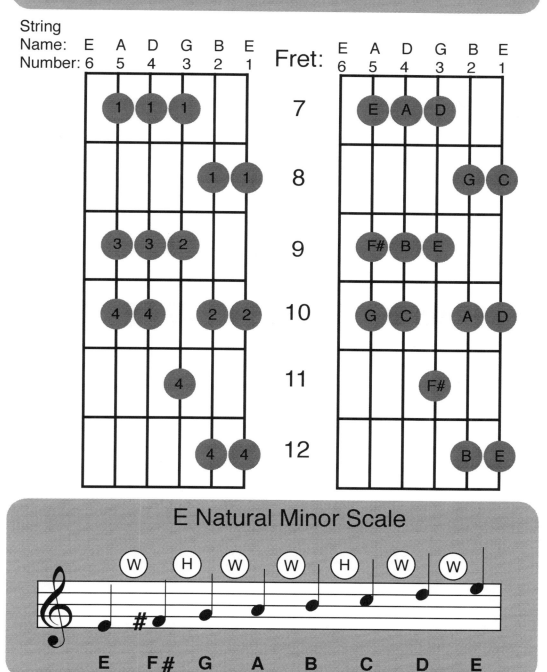

E Natural Minor Scale

Lesson 48: E Harmonic Minor: 5th String, 7th Fret

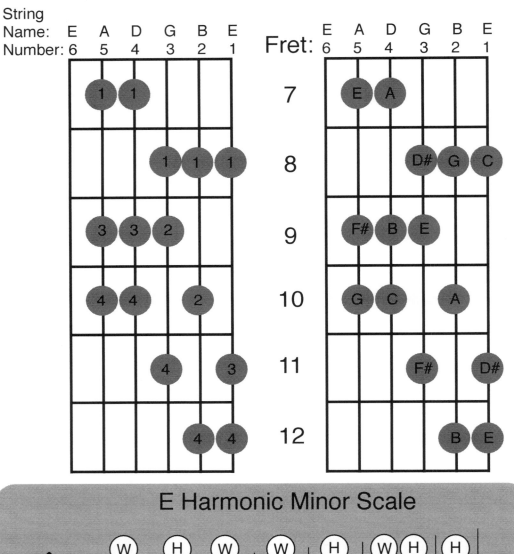

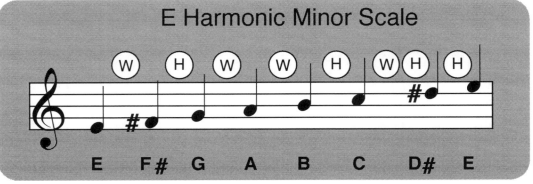

E Harmonic Minor Scale

E F# G A B C D# E

Lesson 49: E Melodic Minor: Ascending: 5th String, 7th Fret

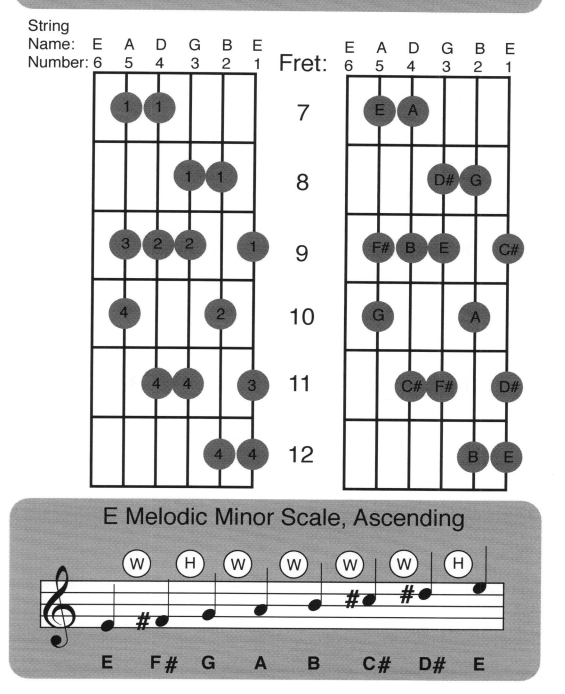

E Melodic Minor Scale, Ascending

Lesson 50: E Melodic Minor: Descending: 5th String, 7th Fret

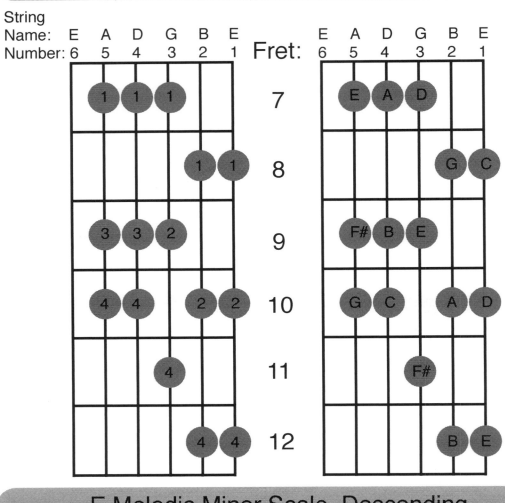

E Melodic Minor Scale, Descending

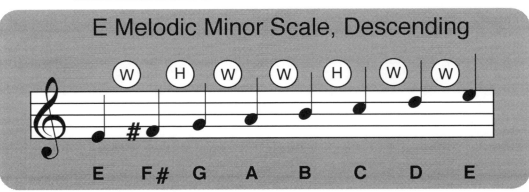

Section

7

Pentatonic Major Scale & Modes Starting on the 6th String

Lesson 51: Pentatonic Major: Introduction & Modes

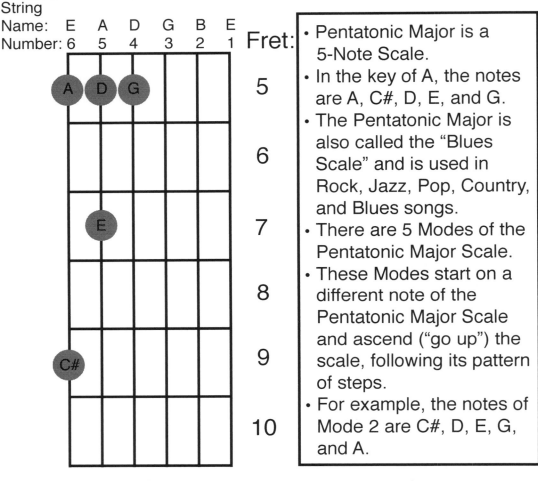

String
Name: E A D G B E
Number: 6 5 4 3 2 1

Fret:
5
6
7
8
9
10

- Pentatonic Major is a 5-Note Scale.
- In the key of A, the notes are A, C#, D, E, and G.
- The Pentatonic Major is also called the "Blues Scale" and is used in Rock, Jazz, Pop, Country, and Blues songs.
- There are 5 Modes of the Pentatonic Major Scale.
- These Modes start on a different note of the Pentatonic Major Scale and ascend ("go up") the scale, following its pattern of steps.
- For example, the notes of Mode 2 are C#, D, E, G, and A.

A Pentatonic Major Notes

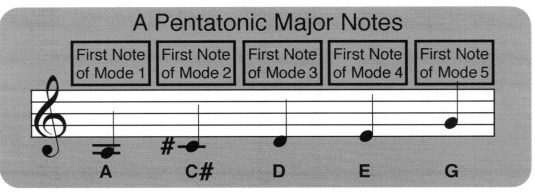

| First Note of Mode 1 | First Note of Mode 2 | First Note of Mode 3 | First Note of Mode 4 | First Note of Mode 5 |

A   C#   D   E   G

Lesson 52: A Pentatonic Major: Mode 1: 6th String, 5th Fret

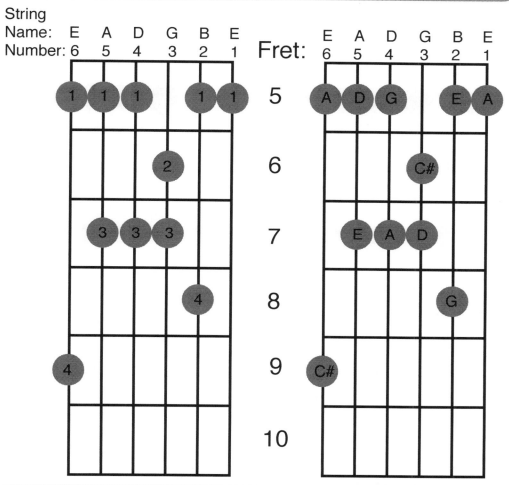

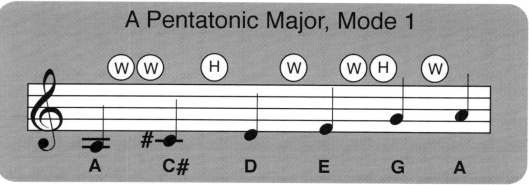

A Pentatonic Major, Mode 1

Lesson 53: A Pentatonic Major: Mode 2: 6th String, 9th Fret

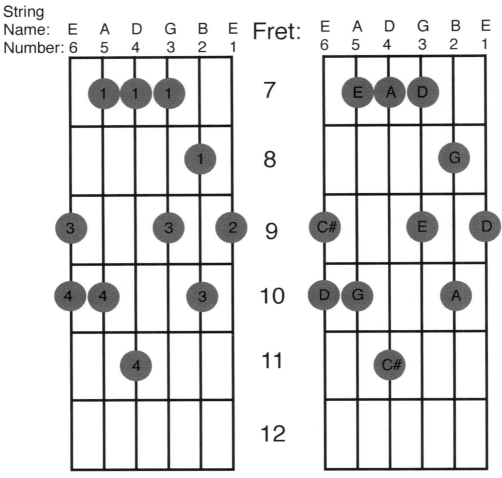

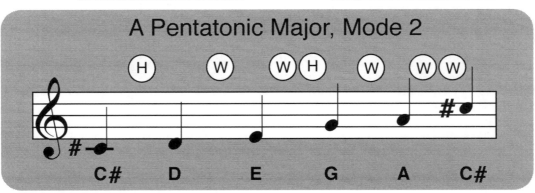

A Pentatonic Major, Mode 2

Lesson 54: A Pentatonic Major: Mode 3: 6th String, 10th Fret

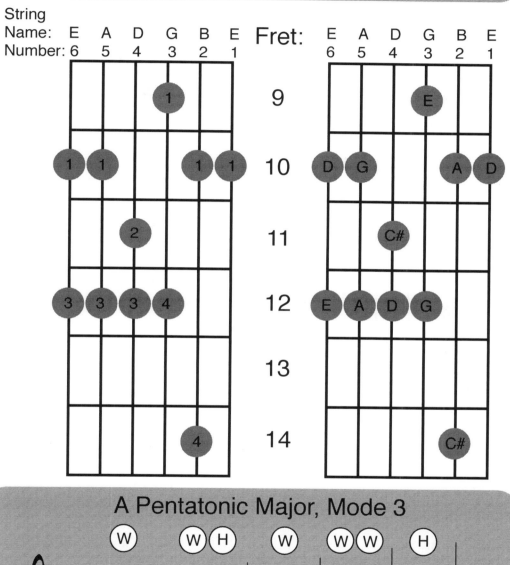

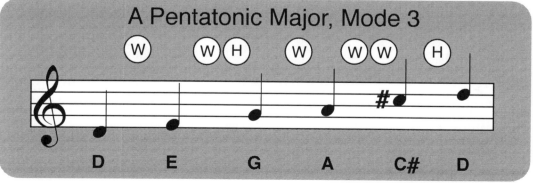

A Pentatonic Major, Mode 3

Lesson 55: A Pentatonic Major: Mode 4: 6th String, 12th Fret

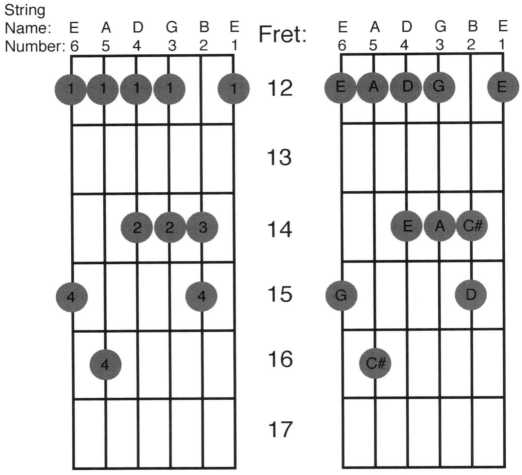

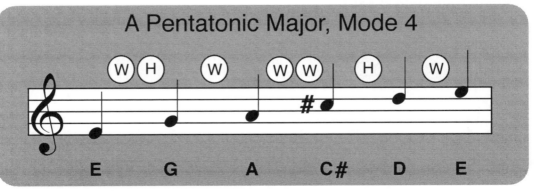

A Pentatonic Major, Mode 4

Lesson 56: A Pentatonic Major: Mode 5: 6th String, 15th Fret

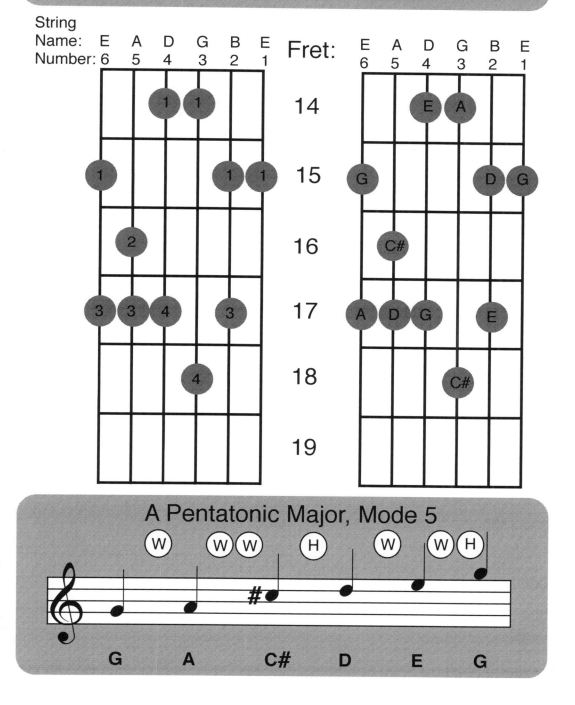

Lesson 57: A Pentatonic Major: Mode 1: 6th String, 17th Fret

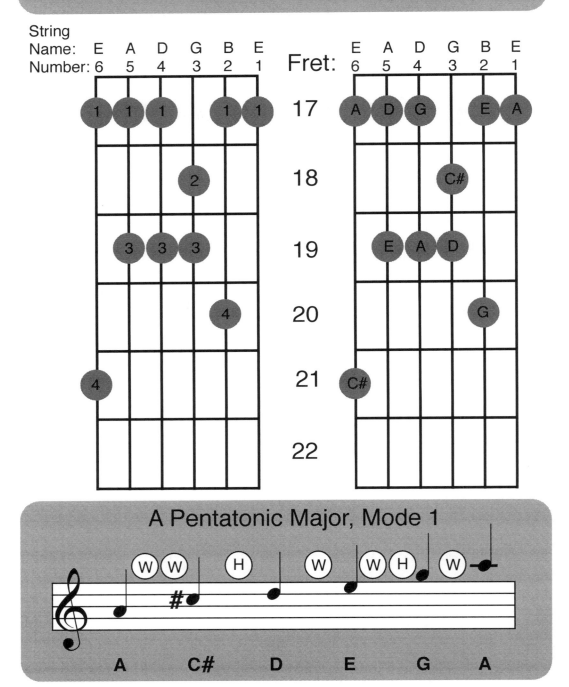

A Pentatonic Major, Mode 1

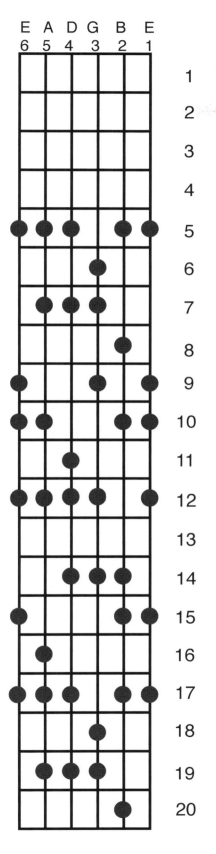

E A D G B E
6 5 4 3 2 1

1
2
3
4
5
6
7
8
9
10
11
12
13
14
15
16
17
18
19
20

Lesson 58: A Pentatonic Major Notes on the Entire Guitar Neck

- The Chart on the left shows all of the notes of the A Pentatonic Major Scale that we have learned in this section of the book.

- Take some time studying this chart and naming its notes on the neck. After you name a note, place your finger on the fret for that note. Repeat this process several times over the course of a few days or a week or two.

- Name the notes of each Mode of Pentatonic Major and find them on the neck.

- Take your time and have fun!

- **Check Out Jam Track Video 7: A Pentatonic Major!**

Section

8

Pentatonic Major
Scale & Modes
Starting on the
5th String

Lesson 59: D Pentatonic Major: Mode 1: 5th String, 5th Fret

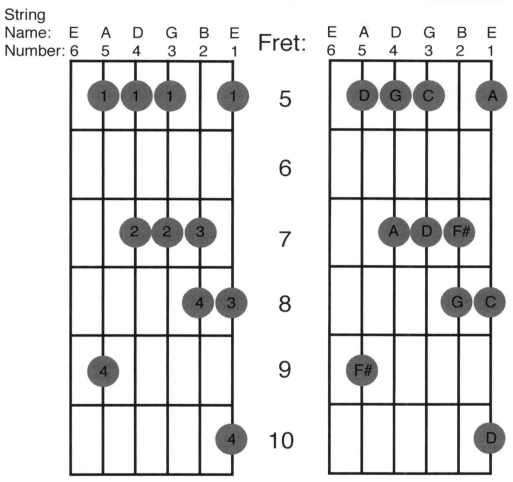

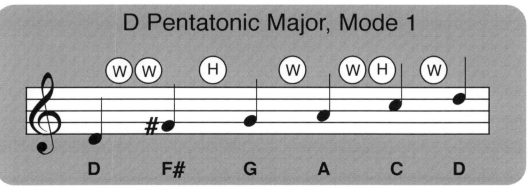

D Pentatonic Major, Mode 1

Lesson 60: D Pentatonic Major: Mode 2: 5th String, 9th Fret

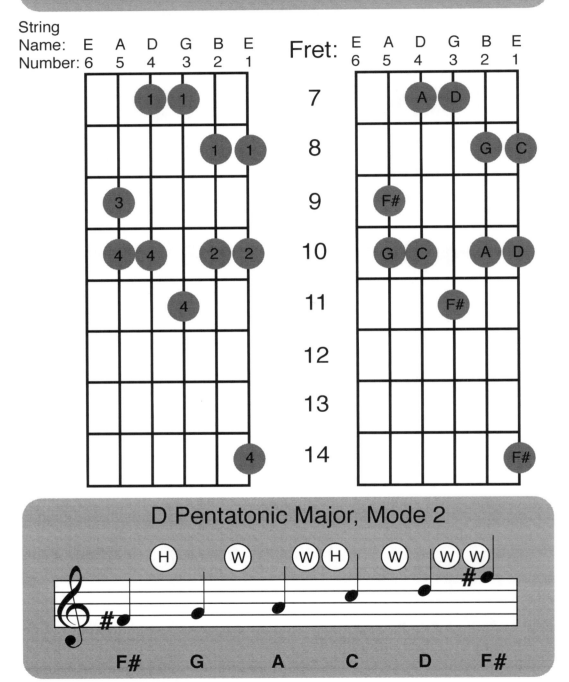

D Pentatonic Major, Mode 2

Lesson 61: D Pentatonic Major: Mode 3: 5th String, 10th Fret

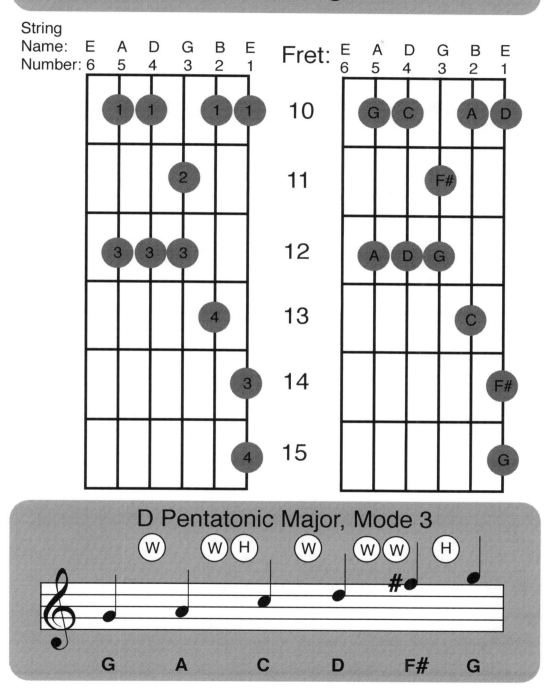

D Pentatonic Major, Mode 3

Lesson 62: D Pentatonic Major: Mode 4: 5th String, 12th Fret

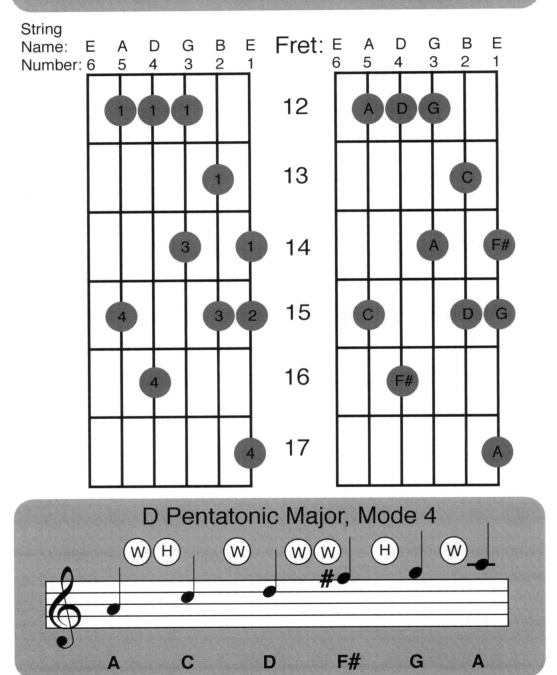

D Pentatonic Major, Mode 4

Lesson 63: D Pentatonic Major: Mode 5: 5th String, 15th Fret

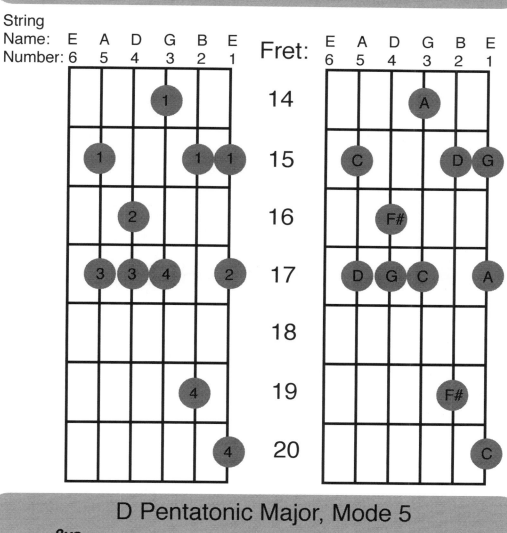

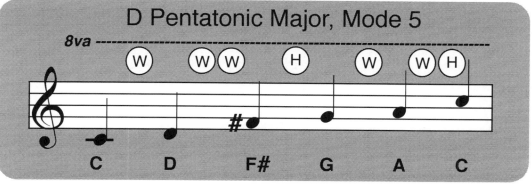

D Pentatonic Major, Mode 5

Lesson 64: D Pentatonic Major: Mode 1: 5th String, 17th Fret

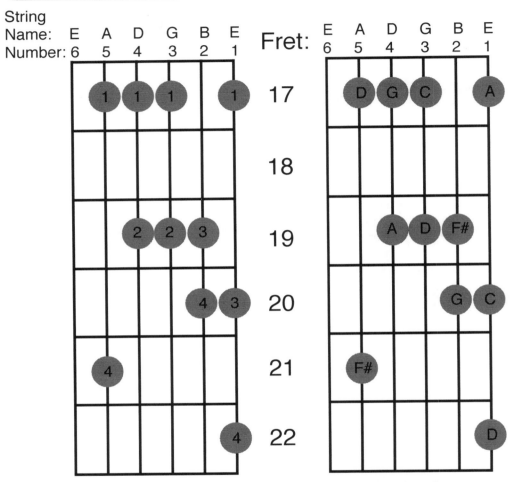

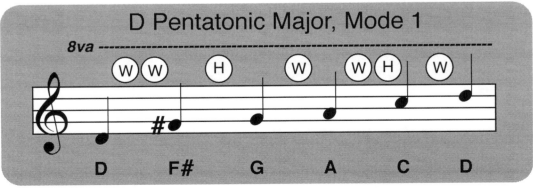

D Pentatonic Major, Mode 1

8va

W W   H   W   W H   W

D   F#   G   A   C   D

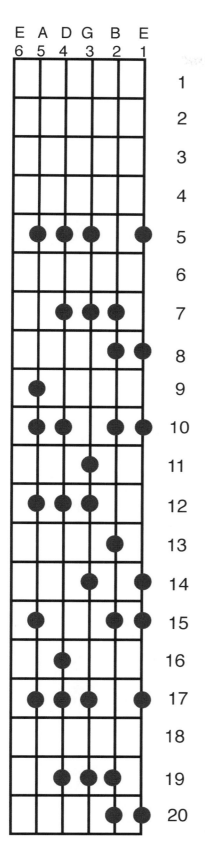

Lesson 65: D Pentatonic Major Notes on the Entire Guitar Neck

- The Chart on the left shows the notes of the D Pentatonic Major Scale that we have learned in this section of the book.

- Take some time studying this chart and naming its notes on the neck. After you name a note, place your finger on the fret for that note. Repeat this process several times over the course of a few days or a week or two.

- Name the notes of each Mode of D Pentatonic Major and find them on the neck.

Section

9

Chromatic Scale Starting on the 5th & 6th Strings

Lesson 66: A Chromatic Scale: 6th String, 5th Fret

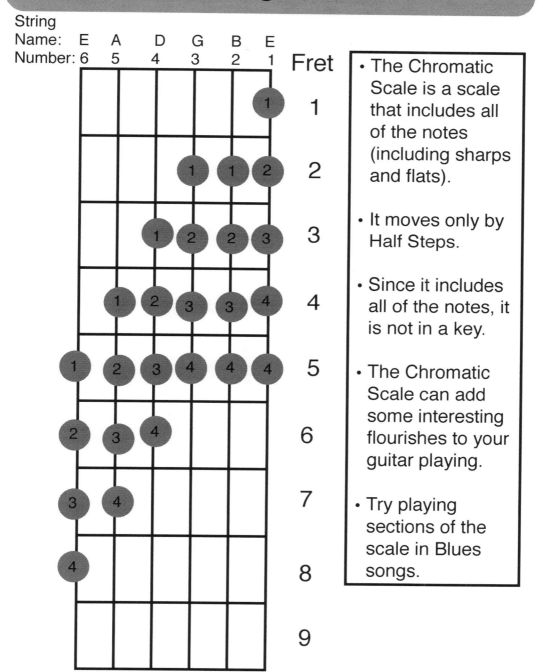

String
Name: E A D G B E
Number: 6 5 4 3 2 1   Fret

- The Chromatic Scale is a scale that includes all of the notes (including sharps and flats).

- It moves only by Half Steps.

- Since it includes all of the notes, it is not in a key.

- The Chromatic Scale can add some interesting flourishes to your guitar playing.

- Try playing sections of the scale in Blues songs.

Section

10

Harmonic Minor
Scale & Modes
Starting on the
6th String

Lesson 67: A Harmonic Minor: Mode 1: 6th String, 5th Fret

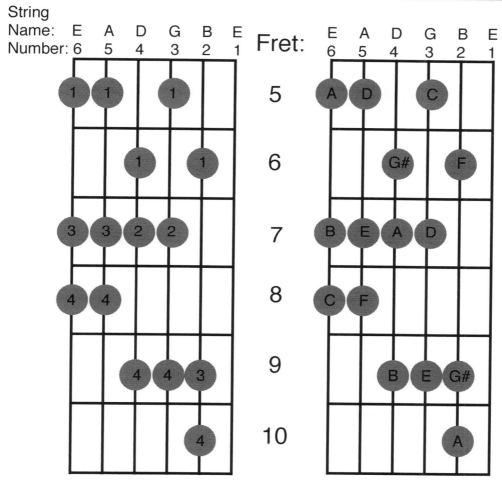

A Harmonic Minor Scale, Mode 1

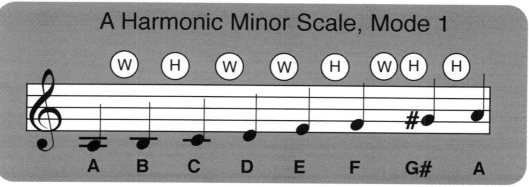

Lesson 68: A Harmonic Minor: Mode 2, 6th String, 7th Fret

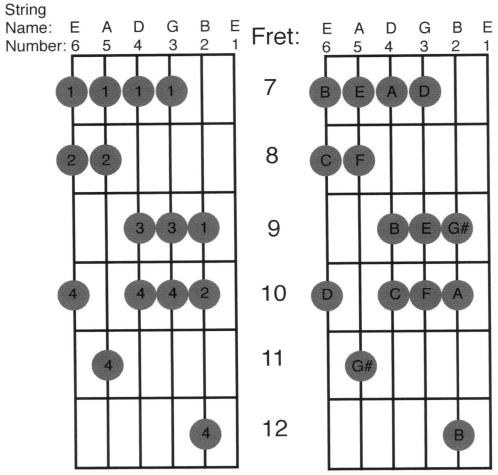

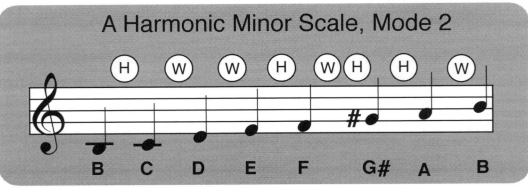

A Harmonic Minor Scale, Mode 2

Lesson 69: A Harmonic Minor: Mode 3, 6th String, 8th Fret

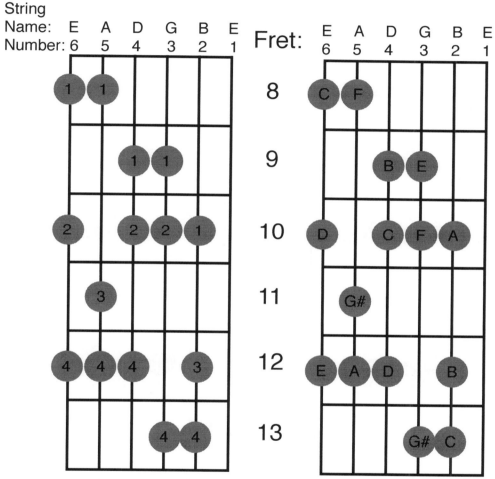

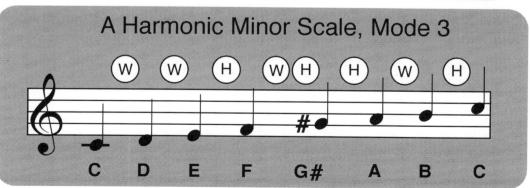

A Harmonic Minor Scale, Mode 3

W W H W H H W H

C D E F G# A B C

Lesson 70: A Harmonic Minor: Mode 4, 6th String, 10th Fret

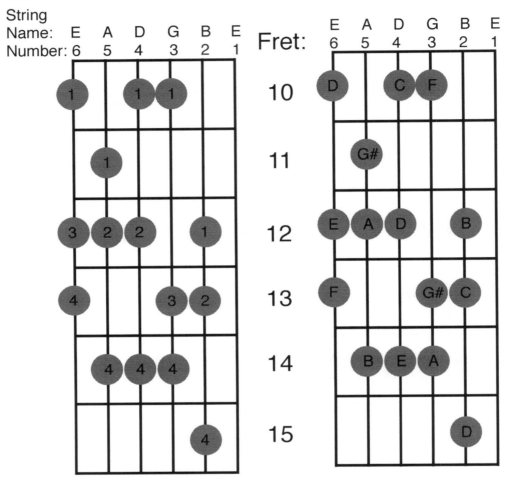

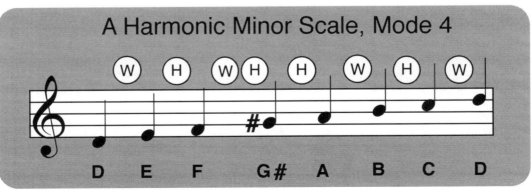

A Harmonic Minor Scale, Mode 4

Lesson 71: A Harmonic Minor: Mode 5, 6th String, 12th Fret

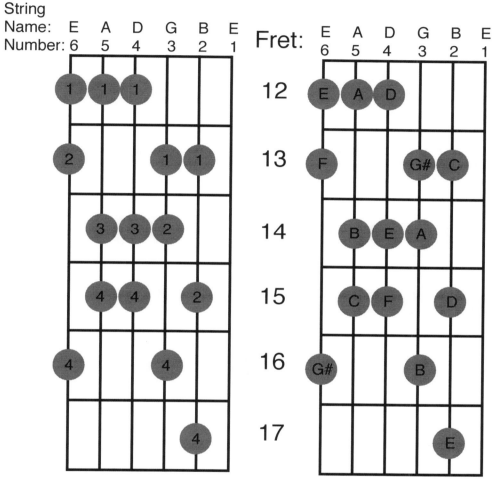

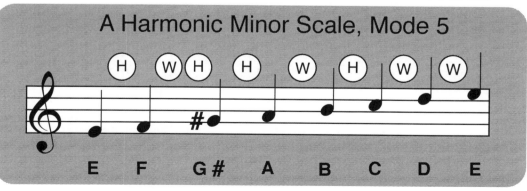

A Harmonic Minor Scale, Mode 5

Lesson 72: A Harmonic Minor: Mode 6, 6th String, 13th Fret

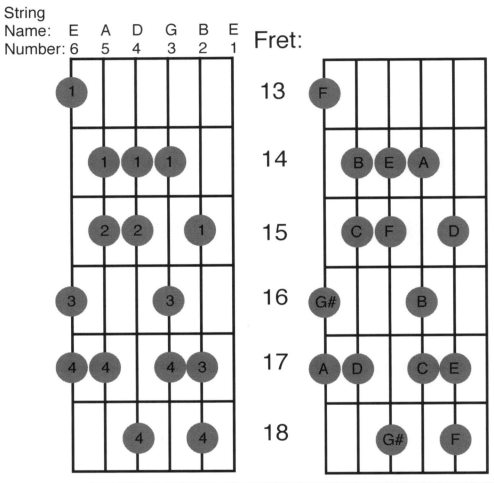

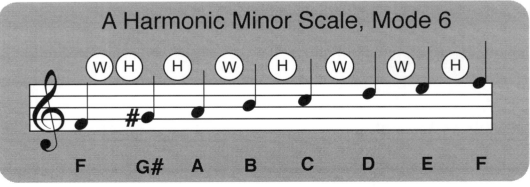

A Harmonic Minor Scale, Mode 6

Lesson 73: A Harmonic Minor: Mode 7, 6th String, 16th Fret

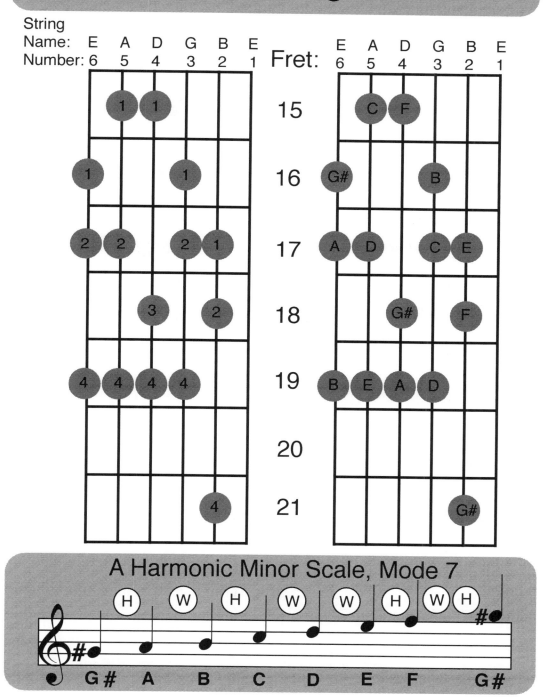

A Harmonic Minor Scale, Mode 7

Lesson 74: A Harmonic Minor: Mode 1, 6th String, 17th Fret

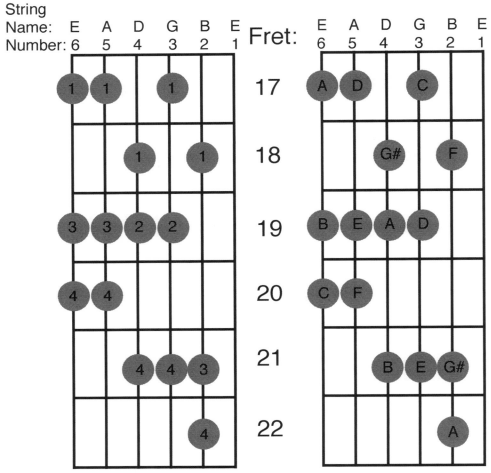

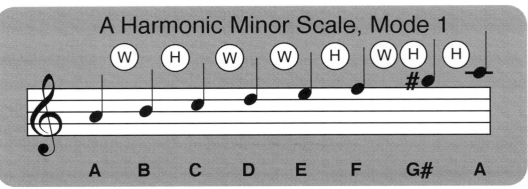

A Harmonic Minor Scale, Mode 1

A B C D E F G# A

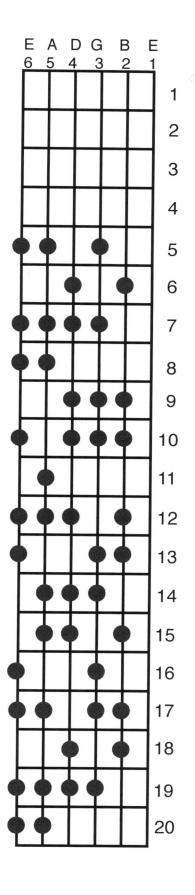

E A D G B E
6 5 4 3 2 1

Lesson 75:
A Harmonic Minor Notes on the Entire Guitar Neck

• The Chart on the left shows the notes of the A Harmonic Minor Scale and Modes that we have learned in this section of the book.

• Take some time studying this chart and naming its notes on the neck. After you name a note, place your finger on the fret for that note. Repeat this process several times over the course of a few days or a week or two.

• If you have made it through these note-naming exercises, so far, you will have made noticeable improvements in your understanding of the notes on the guitar fretboard.

• Good work!

Section

11

Harmonic Minor
Scale & Modes
Starting on the
5th String

Lesson 76: D Harmonic Minor: Mode 1, 5th String, 5th Fret

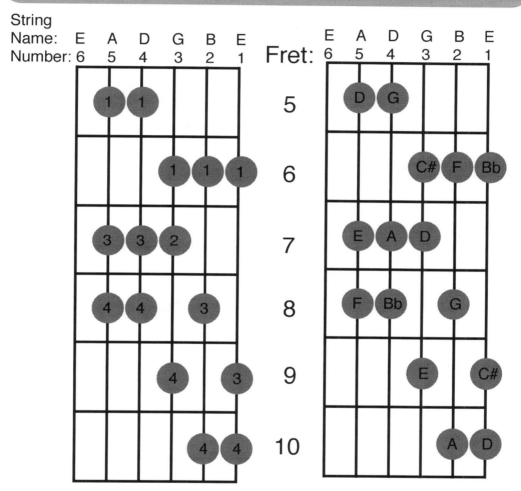

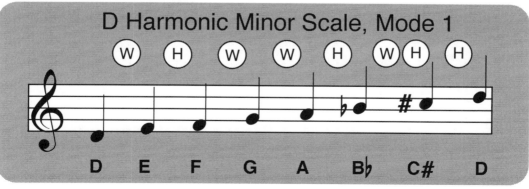

D Harmonic Minor Scale, Mode 1

W H W W H W H H

D E F G A B♭ C# D

Lesson 77: D Harmonic Minor: Mode 2, 5th String, 7th Fret

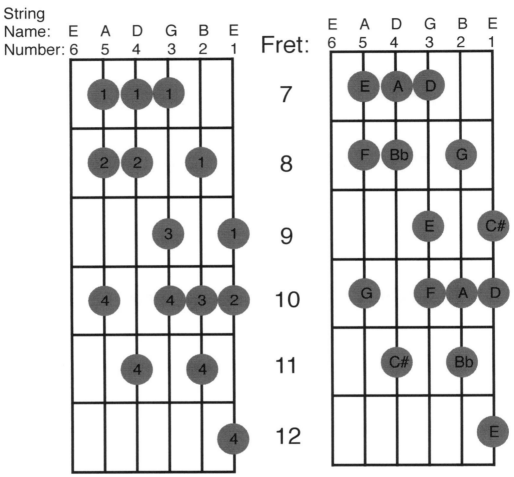

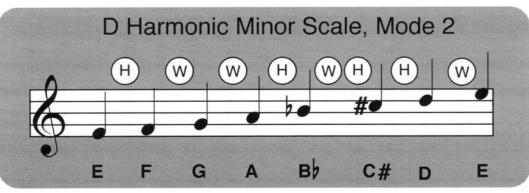

D Harmonic Minor Scale, Mode 2

Lesson 78: D Harmonic Minor: Mode 3, 5th String, 8th Fret

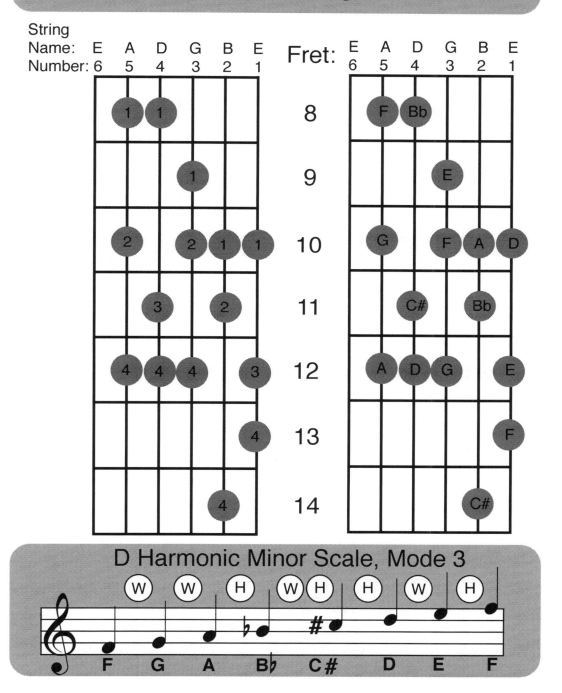

D Harmonic Minor Scale, Mode 3

Lesson 79: D Harmonic Minor: Mode 4, 5th String, 10th Fret

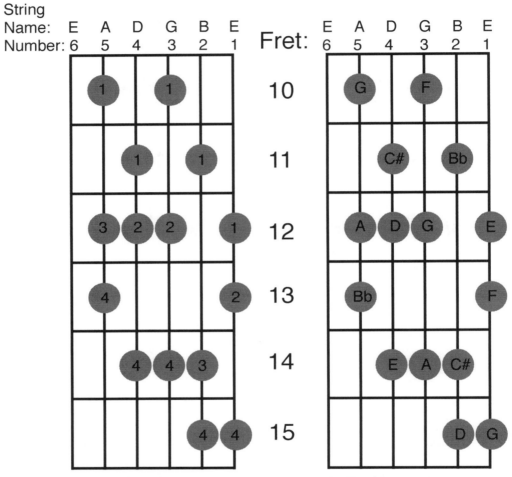

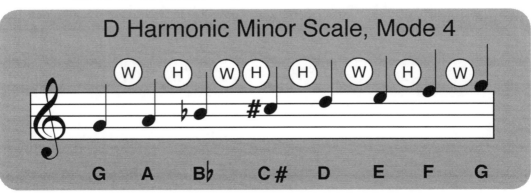

D Harmonic Minor Scale, Mode 4

Lesson 80: D Harmonic Minor: Mode 5, 5th String, 12th Fret

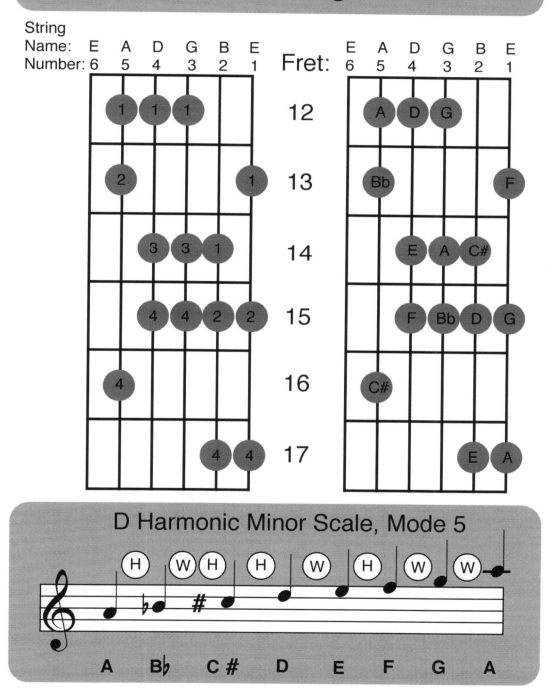

D Harmonic Minor Scale, Mode 5

Lesson 81: D Harmonic Minor: Mode 6, 5th String, 13th Fret

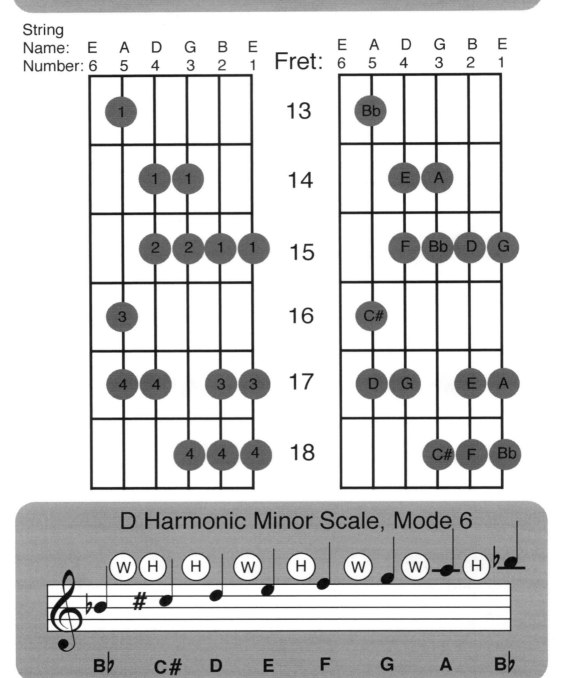

D Harmonic Minor Scale, Mode 6

Lesson 82: D Harmonic Minor: Mode 7, 5th String, 16th Fret

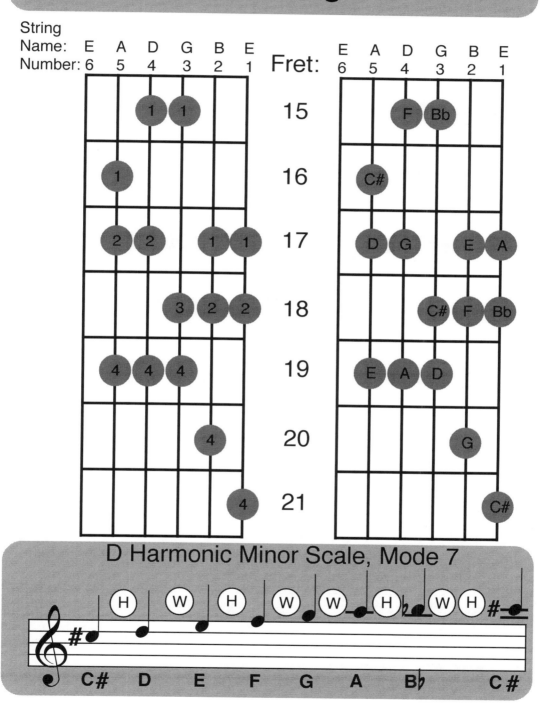

D Harmonic Minor Scale, Mode 7

Lesson 83: D Harmonic Minor: Mode 1, 5th String, 17th Fret

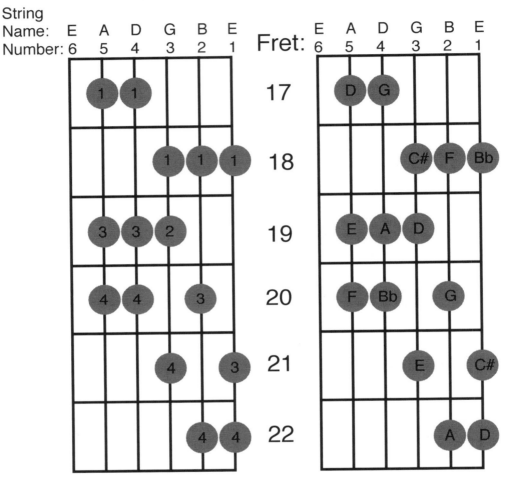

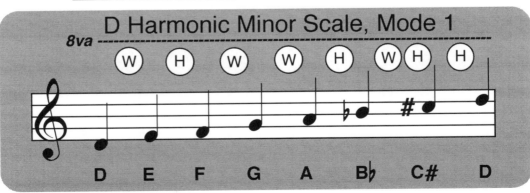

D Harmonic Minor Scale, Mode 1

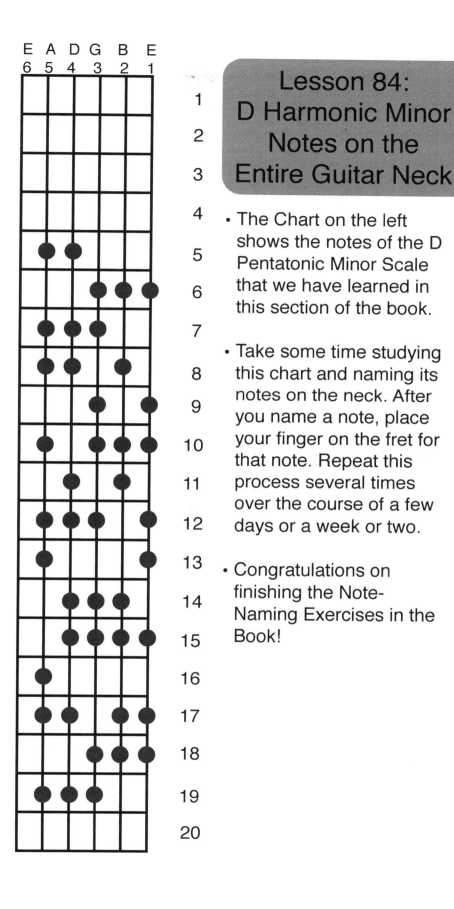

E A D G B E
6 5 4 3 2 1

1
2
3
4
5
6
7
8
9
10
11
12
13
14
15
16
17
18
19
20

Lesson 84: D Harmonic Minor Notes on the Entire Guitar Neck

- The Chart on the left shows the notes of the D Pentatonic Minor Scale that we have learned in this section of the book.

- Take some time studying this chart and naming its notes on the neck. After you name a note, place your finger on the fret for that note. Repeat this process several times over the course of a few days or a week or two.

- Congratulations on finishing the Note-Naming Exercises in the Book!

Section

12

Whole-Tone &
Octatonic Scales
Starting on the
5th & 6th Strings

Lesson 85: A Whole-Tone Scale: 6th String, 5th Fret

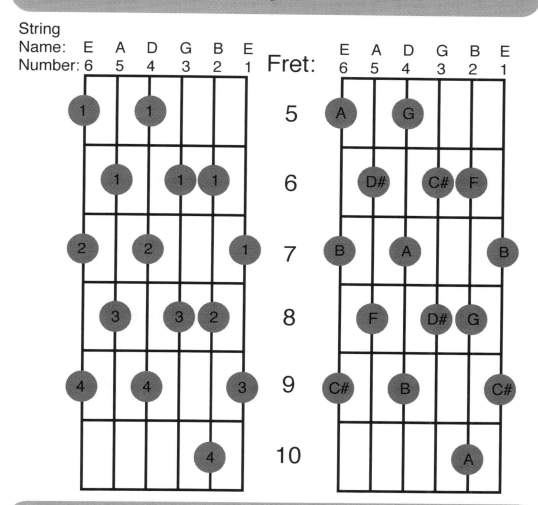

The Whole-Tone Scale

The Whole-Tone Scale is a symmetrical scale whose notes are separated by whole steps. The scale has a "jazzy" avant-garde character.

Lesson 86: D Whole-Tone Scale: 5th String, 5th Fret

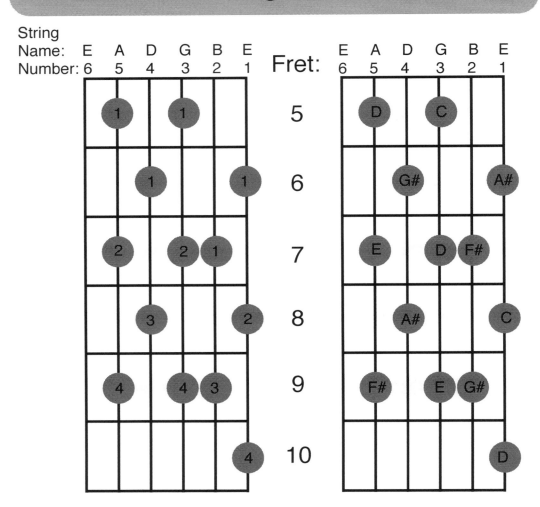

Lesson 87: A Octatonic Scale: 6th String, 5th Fret

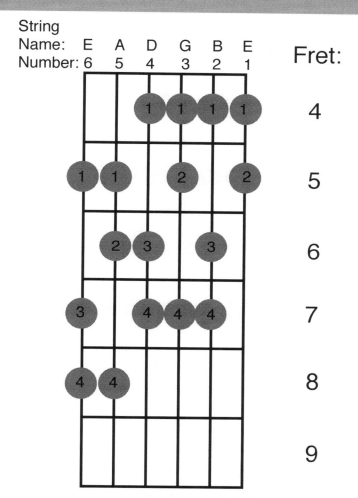

String Name:	E	A	D	G	B	E	Fret:
Number:	6	5	4	3	2	1	

The Octatonic Scale

The Octatonic Scale is also a symmetrical scale. Its notes are separated by alternating whole and half steps. The scale has a "jazzy" avant-garde character, as well.

Lesson 88: C Lydian-Mixolydian: 6th String, 8th Fret

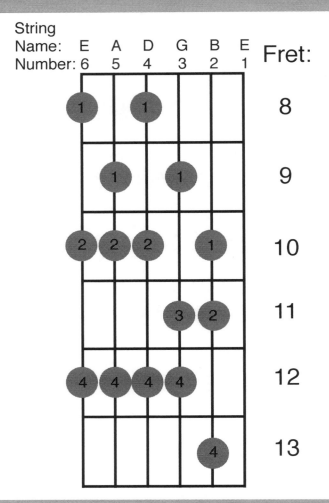

String Name: E A D G B E
Number: 6 5 4 3 2 1

Fret:
8
9
10
11
12
13

C Lydian-Mixolydian Scale

This scale combines the features of the Lydian and Mixolydian Modes. The scale has a "spacey" avant-garde character. Use it to lend an "outside" sound to your blues playing.

Section

13

Three-Octave Scales: Starting on the 6th String

Lesson 89: A Major Scale: 3 Octaves, 6th String, 5th Fret

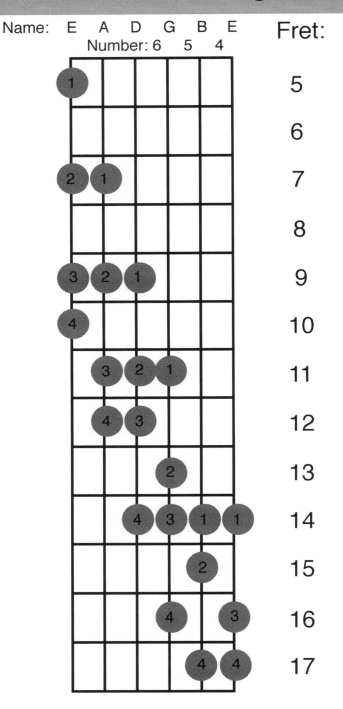

Lesson 90: A Dorian Scale: 3 Octaves, 6th String, 5th Fret

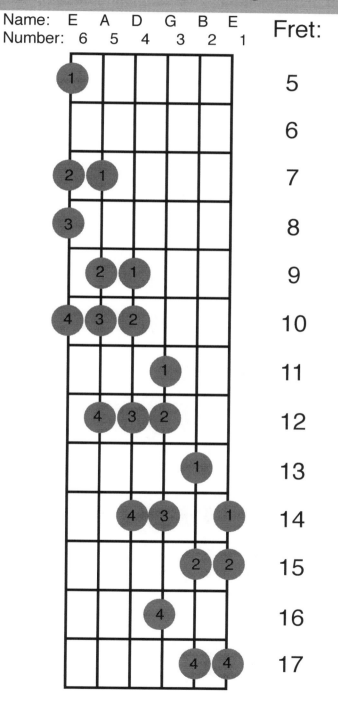

Lesson 91: A Phrygian Scale: 3 Octaves, 6th String, 5th Fret

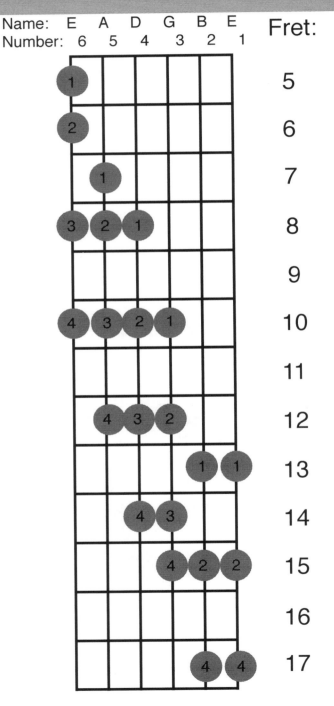

Lesson 92: A Lydian Scale: 3 Octaves, 6th String, 5th Fret

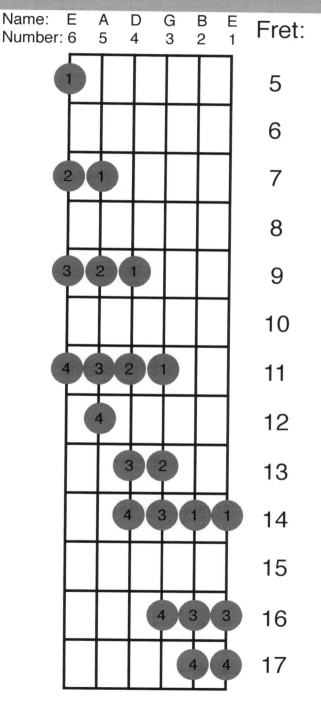

Lesson 93: A Mixolydian Scale: 3 Octaves, 6th String, 5th Fret

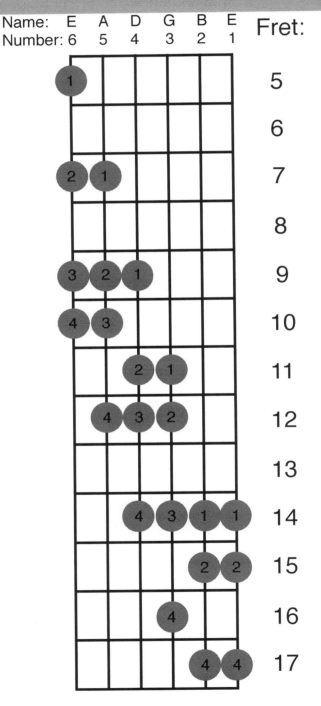

Lesson 94: A Natural Minor Scale: 3 Octaves, 6th String, 5th Fret

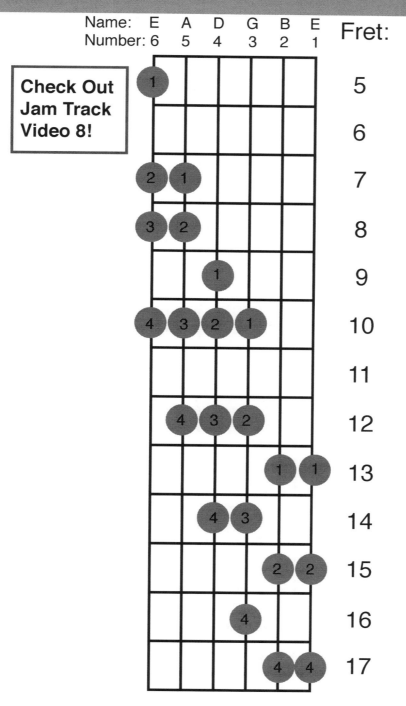

Lesson 95: A Locrian Scale: 3 Octaves, 6th String, 5th Fret

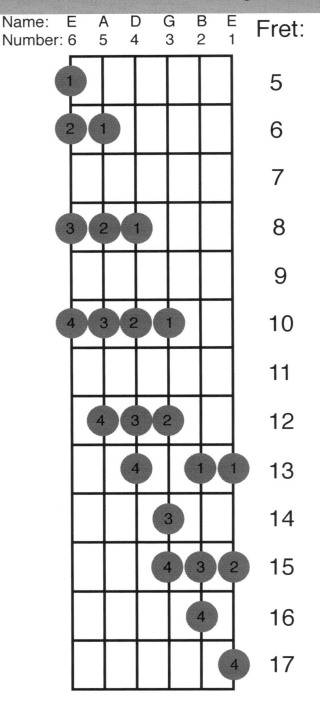

Lesson 96: A Pentatonic Minor: 3 Octaves, 6th String, 5th Fret

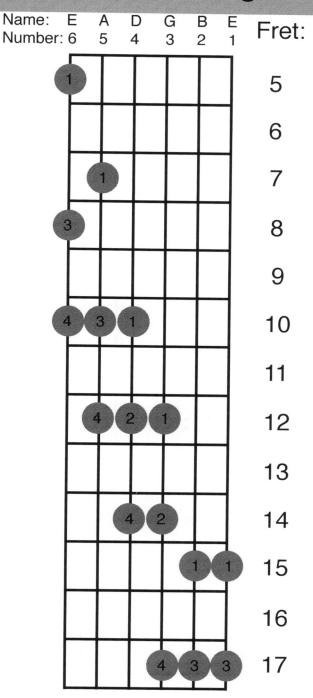

Lesson 97: A Pentatonic Major: 3 Octaves, 6th String, 5th Fret

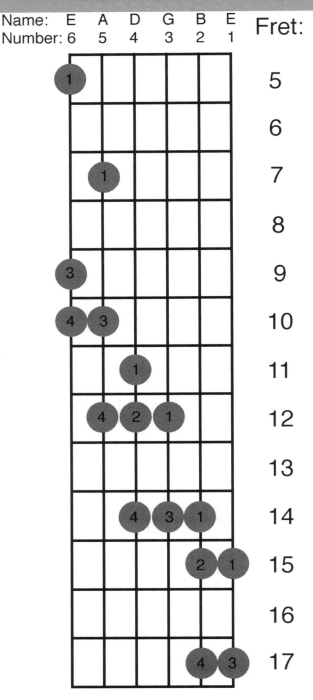

Lesson 98: A Harmonic Minor: 3 Octaves, 6th String, 5th Fret

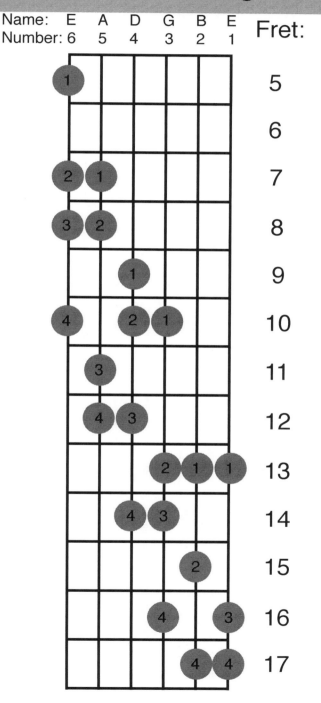

Lesson 99: A Melodic Minor, Ascending: 3 Octaves, 6th String, 5th Fret

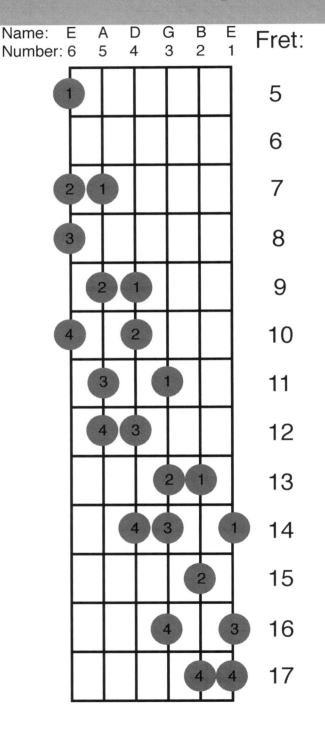

Lesson 100: A Melodic Minor, Descending: 3 Octaves, 6th String, 5th Fret

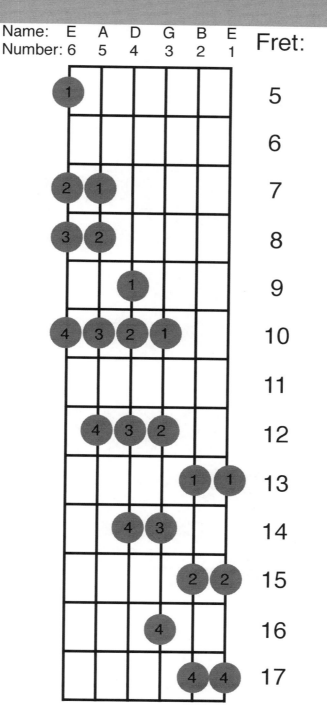

Guitar Chords

Lesson 1: Open Major Chords

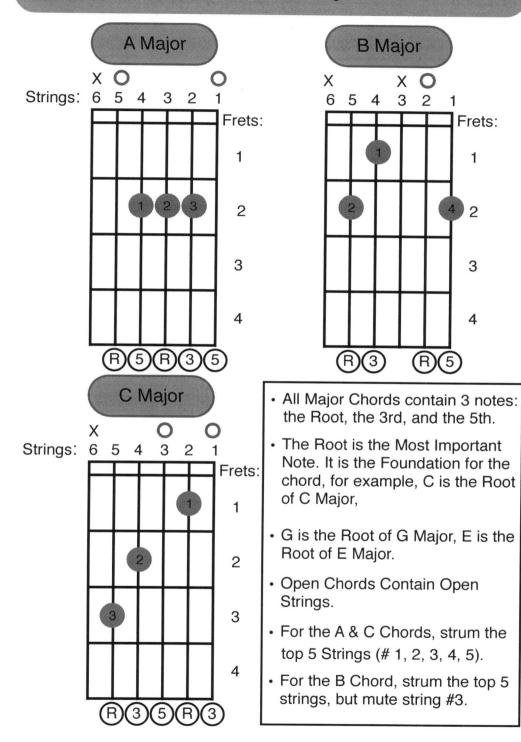

A Major

Strings: 6 5 4 3 2 1

X O   O

Frets: 1 2 3 4

R 5 R 3 5

B Major

6 5 4 3 2 1

X   X O

Frets: 1 2 3 4

R 3   R 5

C Major

Strings: 6 5 4 3 2 1

X   O O

Frets: 1 2 3 4

R 3 5 R 3

- All Major Chords contain 3 notes: the Root, the 3rd, and the 5th.

- The Root is the Most Important Note. It is the Foundation for the chord, for example, C is the Root of C Major,

- G is the Root of G Major, E is the Root of E Major.

- Open Chords Contain Open Strings.

- For the A & C Chords, strum the top 5 Strings (# 1, 2, 3, 4, 5).

- For the B Chord, strum the top 5 strings, but mute string #3.

Lesson 2: Open Major Chords

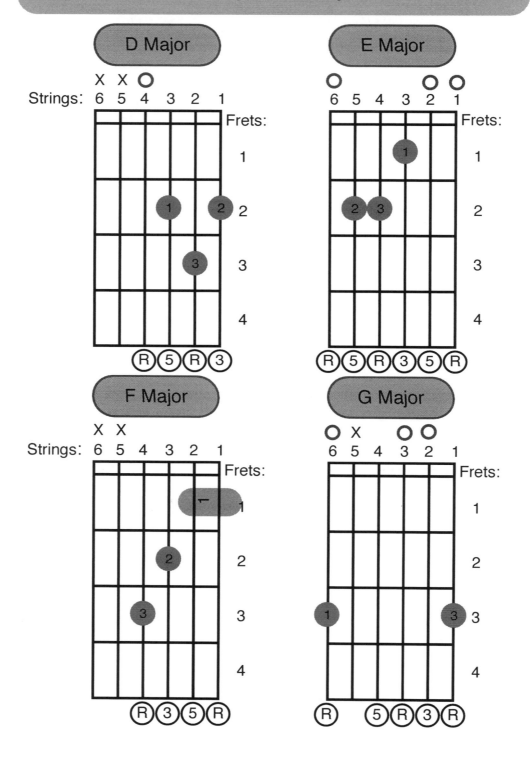

Lesson 3: Open Minor Chords

A Minor

Strings: X O
6 5 4 3 2 1

Frets:

1

2

3

4

(R)(5)(R)(3)(5)

B Minor

X X
6 5 4 3 2 1

Frets:

1

2

3

4

(5)(R)(3)(5)

C Minor

X X
6 5 4 3 2 1

Frets:

2

3

4

5

(5)(R)(3)(5)

Major & Minor Chords

All Major & Minor Chords contain 3 notes: the Root, the 3rd, and the 5th.

In Major Chords the distance between the Root and the 3rd is made up of 2 Major 2nds.

In Minor Chords the distance between the Root and the 3rd is made up of 1 Major 2nd and 1 Minor 2nd.

Lesson 4: Open Minor Chords

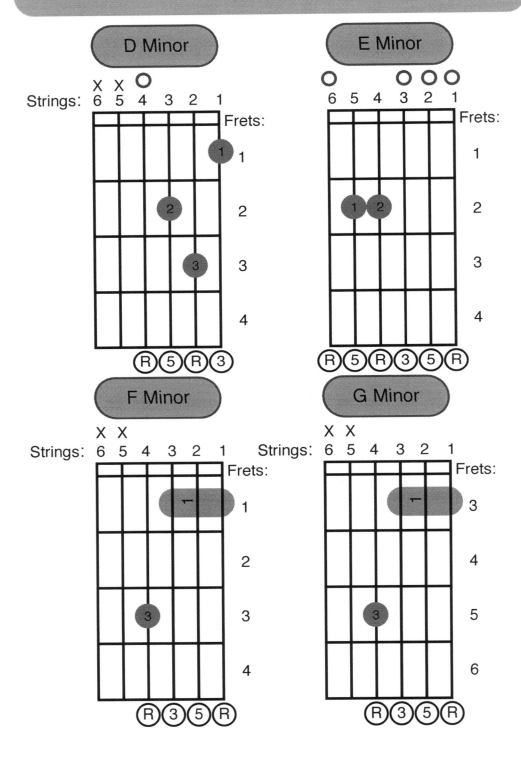

Lesson 5: Open Dominant 7th Chords

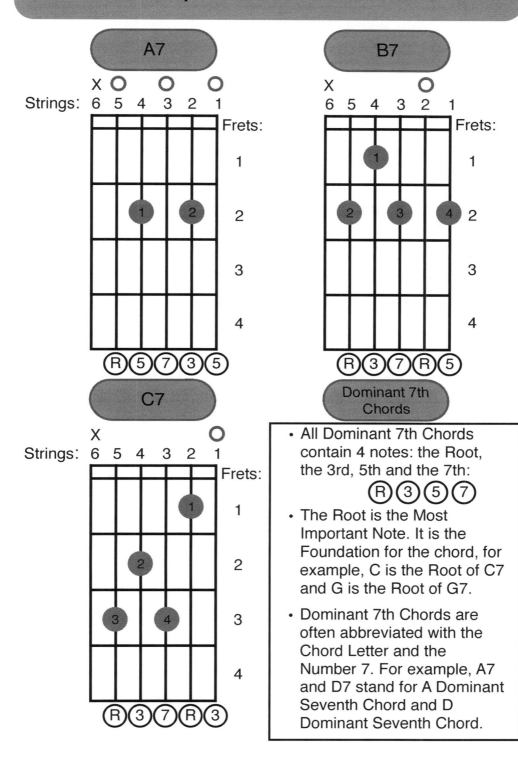

A7

Strings: 6 5 4 3 2 1
X O   O   O

Frets:
1
2
3
4

(R)(5)(7)(3)(5)

B7

Strings: 6 5 4 3 2 1
X   O

Frets:
1
2
3
4

(R)(3)(7)(R)(5)

C7

Strings: 6 5 4 3 2 1
X   O

Frets:
1
2
3
4

(R)(3)(7)(R)(3)

Dominant 7th Chords

- All Dominant 7th Chords contain 4 notes: the Root, the 3rd, 5th and the 7th:

  (R)(3)(5)(7)

- The Root is the Most Important Note. It is the Foundation for the chord, for example, C is the Root of C7 and G is the Root of G7.

- Dominant 7th Chords are often abbreviated with the Chord Letter and the Number 7. For example, A7 and D7 stand for A Dominant Seventh Chord and D Dominant Seventh Chord.

Lesson 6: Open Dominant 7th Chords

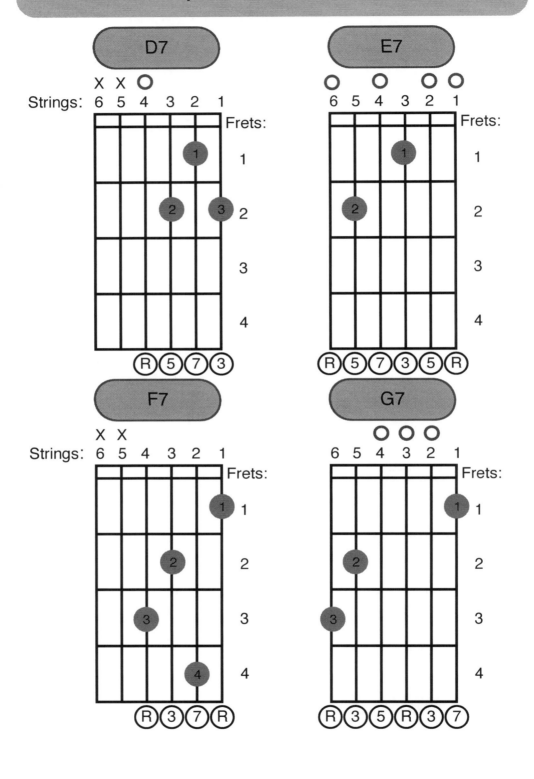

Lesson 7: Open Minor 7th Chords

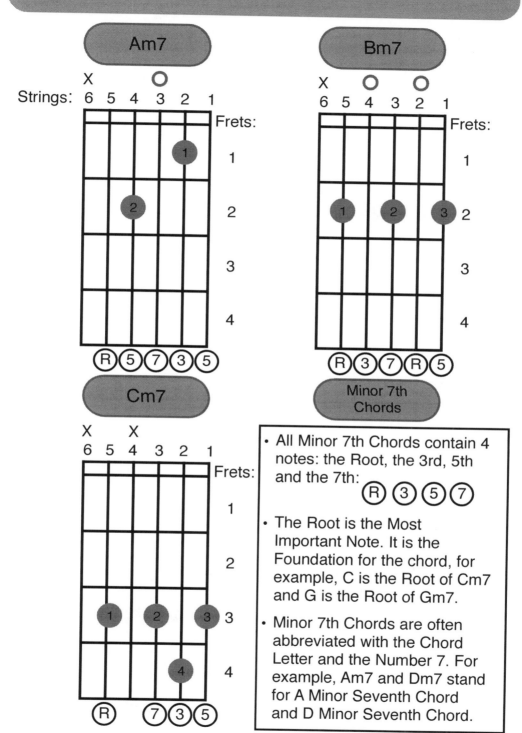

Am7

Strings: 6 5 4 3 2 1
X   O

Frets: 1 2 3 4

R 5 7 3 5

Bm7

6 5 4 3 2 1
X   O   O

Frets: 1 2 3 4

R 3 7 R 5

Cm7

6 5 4 3 2 1
X   X

Frets: 1 2 3 4

R 7 3 5

Minor 7th Chords

- All Minor 7th Chords contain 4 notes: the Root, the 3rd, 5th and the 7th:

  R 3 5 7

- The Root is the Most Important Note. It is the Foundation for the chord, for example, C is the Root of Cm7 and G is the Root of Gm7.

- Minor 7th Chords are often abbreviated with the Chord Letter and the Number 7. For example, Am7 and Dm7 stand for A Minor Seventh Chord and D Minor Seventh Chord.

Lesson 8: Open Minor 7th Chords

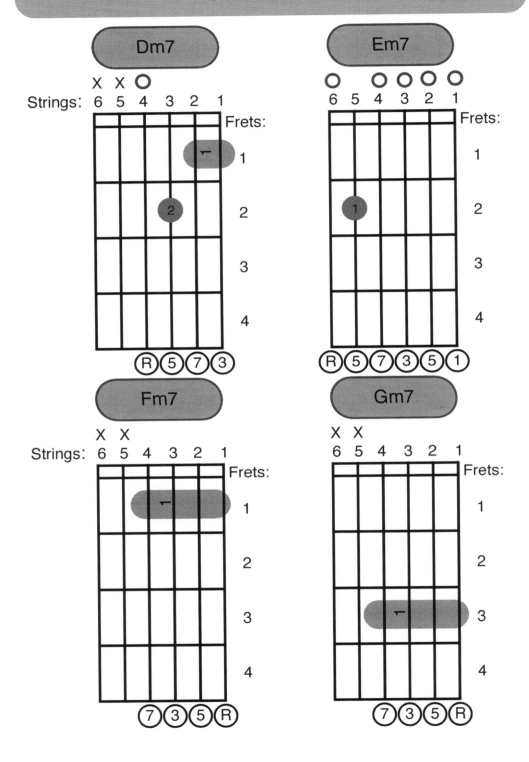

Lesson 9: Open Major 7th Chords

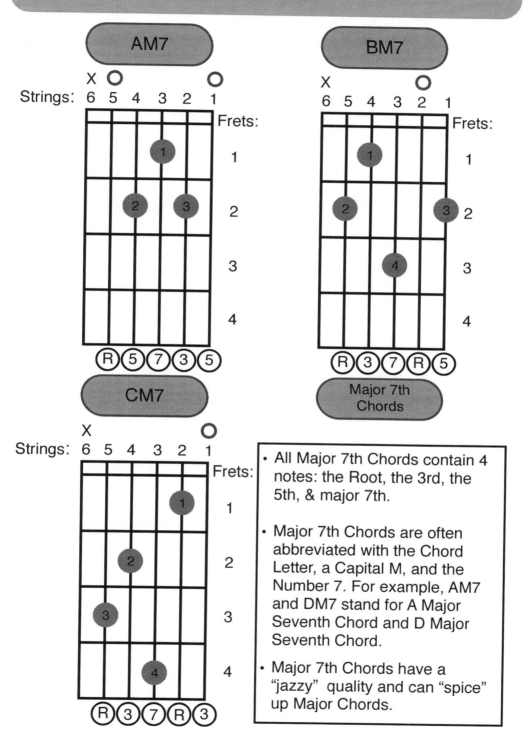

AM7

X O   O
Strings: 6 5 4 3 2 1

Frets:
1
2
3
4

R 5 7 3 5

BM7

X   O
6 5 4 3 2 1

Frets:
1
2
3
4

R 3 7 R 5

CM7

X   O
Strings: 6 5 4 3 2 1

Frets:
1
2
3
4

R 3 7 R 3

Major 7th Chords

- All Major 7th Chords contain 4 notes: the Root, the 3rd, the 5th, & major 7th.

- Major 7th Chords are often abbreviated with the Chord Letter, a Capital M, and the Number 7. For example, AM7 and DM7 stand for A Major Seventh Chord and D Major Seventh Chord.

- Major 7th Chords have a "jazzy" quality and can "spice" up Major Chords.

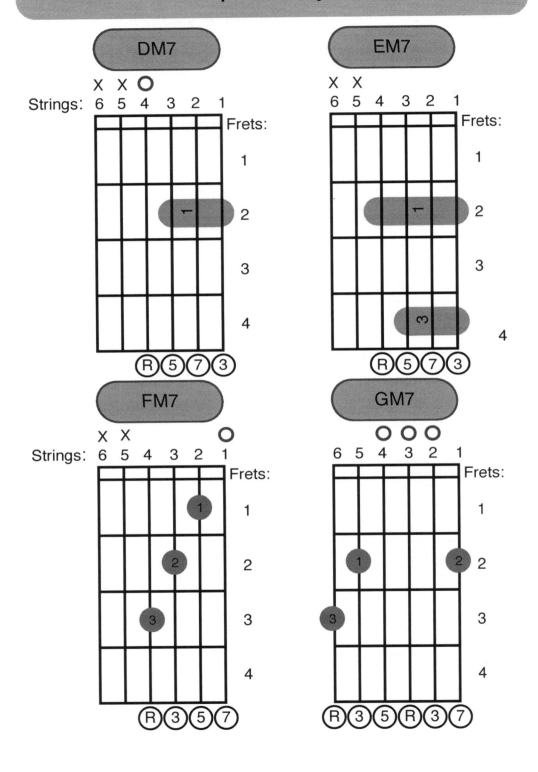

Lesson 10: Open Major 7th Chords

Moveable Chords & Barre Chords

- Moveable Chords allow you to play any Chord by moving your hand to a different fret.

- Check out the Neck Diagram Charts at the beginning of the book for the notes of the neck.

- The chords in this section include the fingering and chord degree.

  (R)   means Root

  (3)   means 3rd

  (5)   means 5th

  (7)   means 7th

  (9)   means 9th

  (11) means 11th

  (13) means 13th

- Barre Chords are Chords where you use your index finger over 5 or 6 strings to help form the Chord Shape.

- Barre Chords are very helpful in creating full-sounding chords in any key.

Lesson 12: Moveable Major Chords

Barre Chord

Strings: 6 5 4 3 2 1

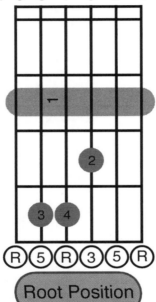

R 5 R 3 5 R

Barre Chord

X

Strings: 6 5 4 3 2 1

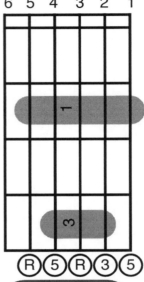

R 5 R 3 5

Root Position

X X

Strings: 6 5 4 3 2 1

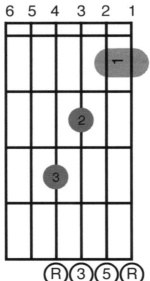

R 3 5 R

Root Position

X   X

Strings: 6 5 4 3 2 1

R 3 5 R

Lesson 13: Moveable Minor Chords

Barre Chord

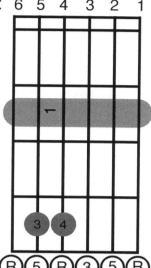

Strings: 6 5 4 3 2 1

R 5 R 3 5 R

Barre Chord

X
6 5 4 3 2 1

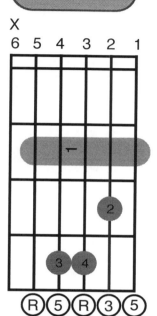

R 5 R 3 5

Root Position

X X
Strings: 6 5 4 3 2 1

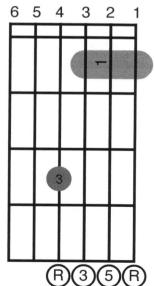

R 3 5 R

Root Position

X   X
6 5 4 3 2 1

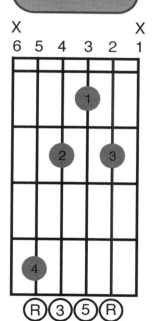

R 3 5 R

Lesson 14: Moveable Sus. 4 Chords

Barre Chord

Strings: 6 5 4 3 2 1

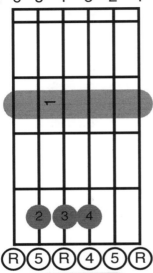

R 5 R 4 5 R

Barre Chord

X
Strings: 6 5 4 3 2 1

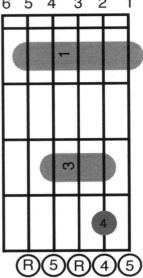

R 5 R 4 5

Root Position

X X
Strings: 6 5 4 3 2 1

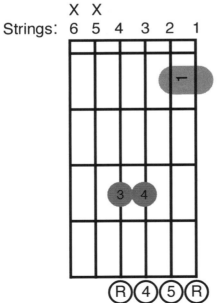

R 4 5 R

Root Position

X   X
Strings: 6 5 4 3 2 1

R 4 5 R

Lesson 15: Moveable Diminished & Augmented Chords

Diminished

```
        X           X
Strings: 6  5  4  3  2  1

              1

           2     3

              4
        (R)(5)(R)(3)
```

Diminished

```
        X  X
Strings: 6  5  4  3  2  1

                    1

                 2     3

              4
           (R)(3)(5)(R)
```

Augmented

```
        X           X
Strings: 6  5  4  3  2  1

                 1  2

              3

        4
        (R)(3)(5)(R)
```

Augmented

```
        X  X
Strings: 6  5  4  3  2  1

                       1

                 2  3

              4
           (R)(3)(5)(R)
```

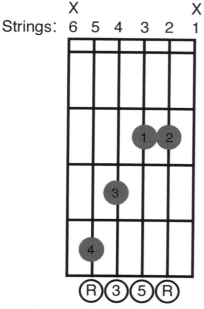
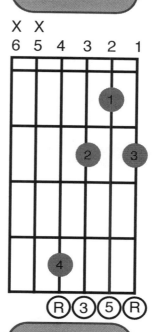

Lesson 16: Moveable Dominant 7th Chords

Barre Chord

Strings: 6 5 4 3 2 1

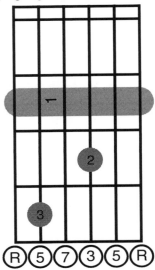

Ⓡ ⑤ ⑦ ③ ⑤ Ⓡ

Barre Chord

X
6 5 4 3 2 1

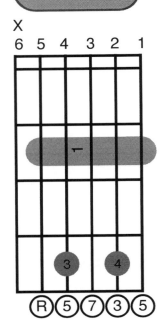

Ⓡ ⑤ ⑦ ③ ⑤

Root Position

X X
Strings: 6 5 4 3 2 1

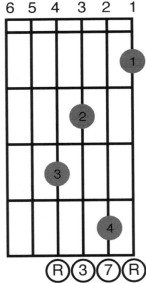

Ⓡ ③ ⑦ Ⓡ

Root Position

X   X
Strings: 6 5 4 3 2 1

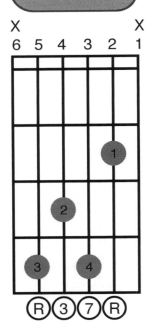

Ⓡ ③ ⑦ Ⓡ

Lesson 17: Moveable Minor 7th Chords

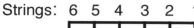

Barre Chord

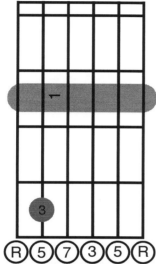

Strings: 6 5 4 3 2 1

(R)(5)(7)(3)(5)(R)

Barre Chord

X

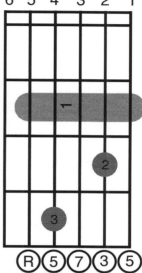

6 5 4 3 2 1

(R)(5)(7)(3)(5)

Root Position

X X

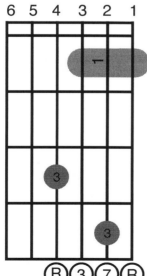

Strings: 6 5 4 3 2 1

(R)(3)(7)(R)

Root Position

X   X

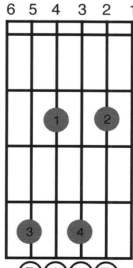

6 5 4 3 2 1

(R)(3)(7)(R)

Lesson 18: Moveable Major 7th Chords

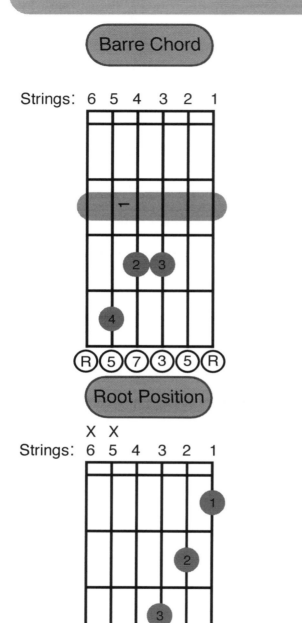

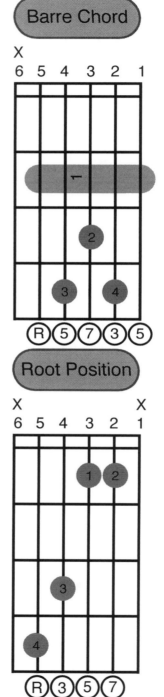

Lesson 19: Chord Families

- The chords in the following lessons can be grouped into 3 basic families: Major, Minor, and Dominant.

- You can substitute chords within each family to add variety to your playing. For example, you may substitute a C Major 7th Chord for a C Major Chord; they are both in the Major Chord Family. You may also, for example, switch a D Augmented 7th Chord for a D Dominant 7th Chord; they are both in the Dominant Chord Family.

- Here is a listing of the Chord Families:

Major Chord Family:

- Major 7th Chords
- Major 6th Chords
- Suspended 4th Chords
- 11th Chords
- 13th Chords

Minor Chord Family:

- Minor 7th Chords
- Minor 6th Chords
- Suspended 4th Chords
- Minor 7th Flat 5 Chords
- Minor 9th Chords
- Minor 11th Chords
- MInor 13th Chords

Dominant Chord Family:

- Dominant 7th Chords
- Dominant 9th Chords
- Augmented 7th Chords
- 11th Chords
- 13th Chords

Lesson 20: Moveable Major 6th Chords

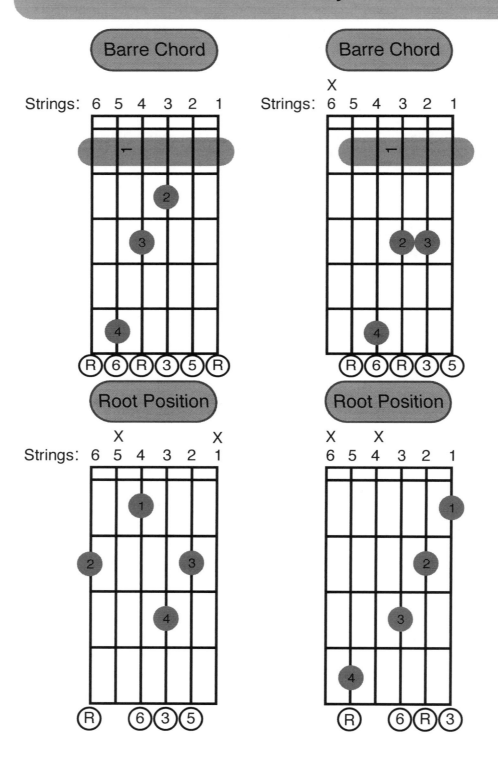

Lesson 21: Moveable Minor 6th Chords

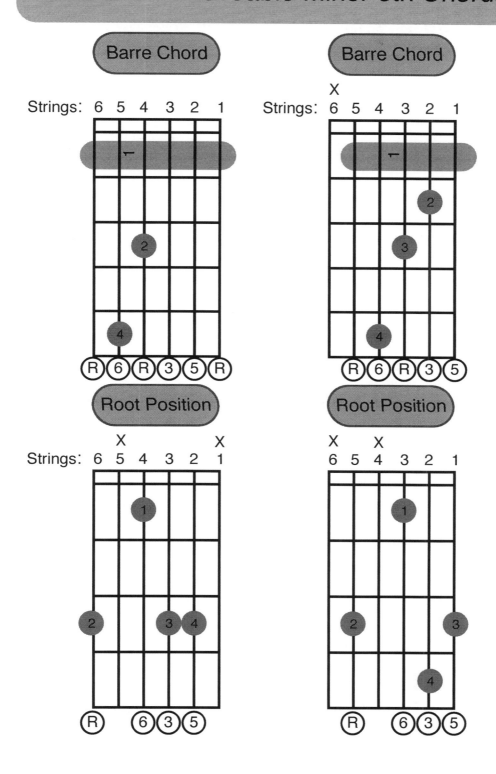

Barre Chord

Strings: 6 5 4 3 2 1

Barre Chord

X
Strings: 6 5 4 3 2 1

Root Position

X   X
Strings: 6 5 4 3 2 1

Root Position

X   X
6 5 4 3 2 1

Lesson 22: Moveable Dominant 9th Chords

Barre Chord

Strings: 6 5 4 3 2 1

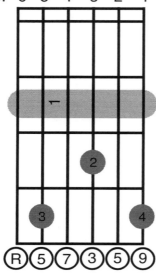

R 5 7 3 5 9

Barre Chord

X
6 5 4 3 2 1

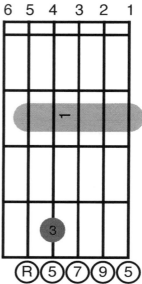

R 5 7 9 5

Root Position

X X
Strings: 6 5 4 3 2 1

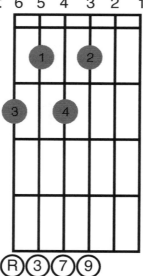

R 3 7 9

Root Position

X
6 5 4 3 2 1

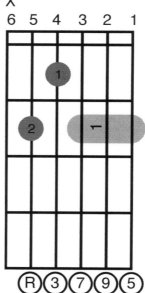

R 3 7 9 5

Lesson 23: Moveable Minor 9th Chords

Barre Chord

Strings: 6 5 4 3 2 1

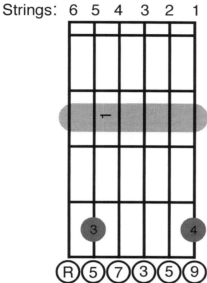

R 5 7 3 5 9

Barre Chord

X
6 5 4 3 2 1

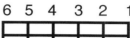
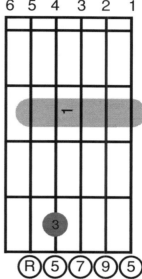

R 5 7 9 5

Root Position

X X
Strings: 6 5 4 3 2 1

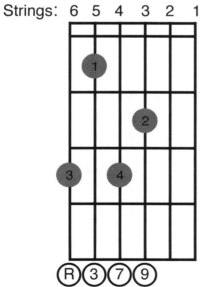

R 3 7 9

Root Position

X
6 5 4 3 2 1

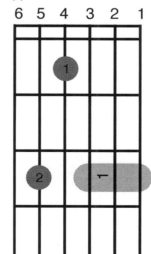

R 3 7 9 5

Lesson 24: Moveable Minor 7th Flat 5 Chords

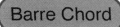

Barre Chord

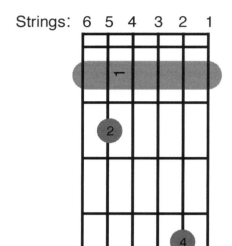

Strings: 6 5 4 3 2 1

(R)(5)(7)(3)(7)(R)

Root Position

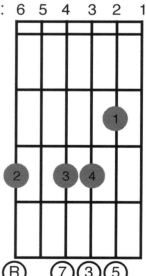

Strings: 6 5 4 3 2 1
X X   X

(R) (7)(3)(5)

Barre Chord

X
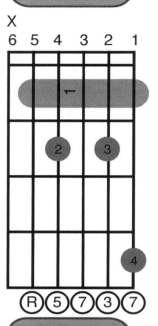

Strings: 6 5 4 3 2 1

(R)(5)(7)(3)(7)

Root Position

X   X
6 5 4 3 2 1

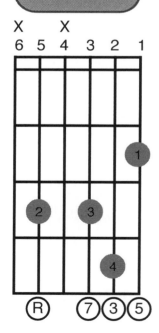

(R) (7)(3)(5)

Lesson 25: Moveable Diminished 7th Chords

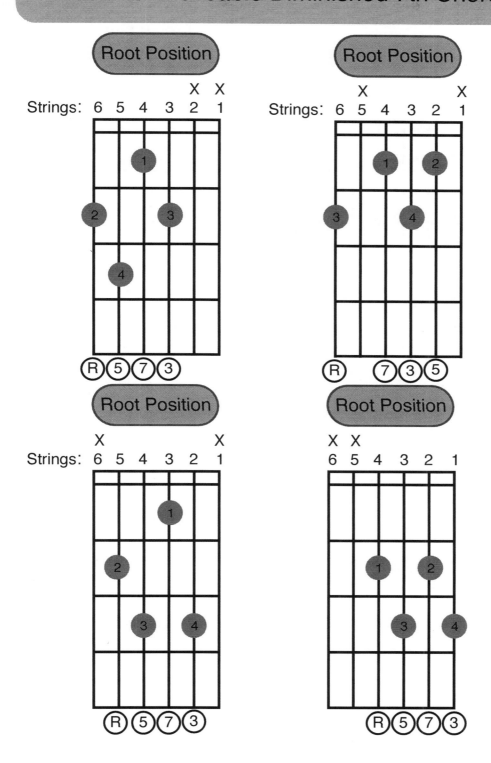

Lesson 26: Moveable Augmented 7th Chords

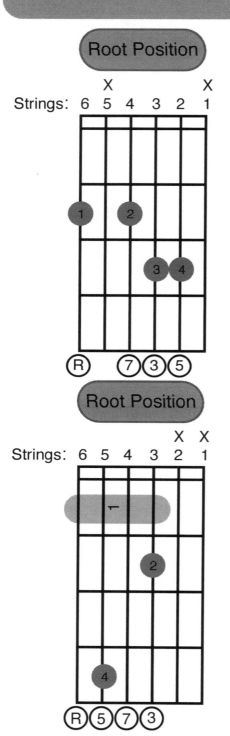

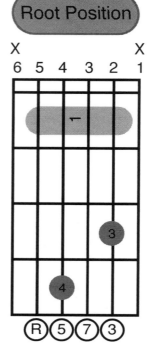

- The Augmented 7th Chord can be used to "spice up" Dominant 7th or Dominant 9th Chords.

- It is great at intensifying the movement from a V7 chord to a I Chord.

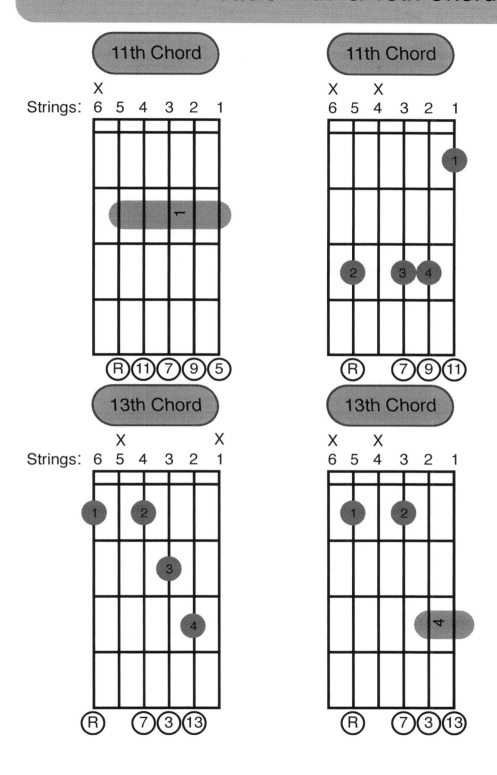

Guitar Arpeggios

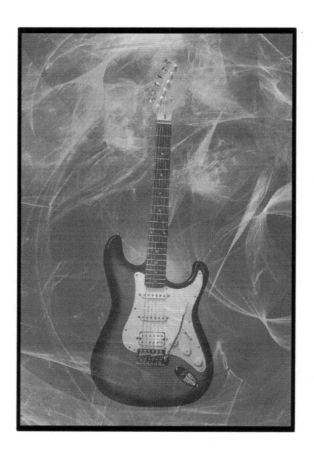

Table of Contents

Introduction:
A Few Words About Arpeggios

- Arpeggios are one of the most exciting, great sounding, and fun elements of music. If you have ever played or listened to the beginning of "Stairway to Heaven", "Sweet Child O' Mine", "Cliffs of Dover", or "Wanted Dead or Alive", you have some experience and understanding of arpeggios. Put simply, arpeggios are chords where the notes sound one at a time, rather than simultaneously.

- Arpeggios are a great feature of music that can add vibrancy, expressivity, and subtlety to your guitar solos, song writing, licks, fills, embellishments, and improvisation.

- These lessons are designed so that you will learn one arpeggio pattern each day (or every few days, depending on your practice schedule) in an easy-to-follow, step-by-step format. The book is progressive, so that you start with the basics and move, little by little, to more complex and sophisticated patterns. By the end of the book you will have picked up over a hundred new arpeggios, as well as some valuable music theory and fretboard theory.

- The first section of the book presents 3-note arpeggios. The second section teaches you 4-note arpeggios (including seventh arpeggios). The third section of the book adds 2-octave arpeggios (including 6th, 7th, 9th, 11th, and 13th arpeggios). The final section of the book provides 3-octave arpeggios, which span most of the guitar neck; these are the most advanced figures.

- Each section of the book contains lessons on music theory. So, you will learn about how these arpeggios are formed and when to use them best over chord progressions in songs and in your song writing.

- There are 7 Play-Along Jam Track Videos that correspond to the arpeggios. These videos let you try out the arpeggio patterns over chord progressions

- Practicing these arpeggios will greatly improve your guitar technique. Some of the arpeggios, especially ones that cover only 2 strings will require some stretching in your left hand. In order to facilitate these stretches, move your left-hand thumb lower behind the guitar neck.

Section

1

3-Note Arpeggios

Lesson 1: Intervals: Music Theory Overview

- "Triads" are 3-note arpeggios and chords. The most common triads are Major and Minor.

- Major and Minor Arpeggios, which can also be called Major and Minor Triads, are composed of Intervals.

- "Intervals" are the distances between two notes in music. For example, the distance between the notes "E" and "F" on your fretboard (the open E string and the 1st fret of the E string) is an interval, which is called a "minor second".

- Here are some common names for intervals: minor second, major third, minor third, perfect 4th, perfect 5th, and octave. While these names may seem a bit technical, they just indicate the space between 2 notes. Try playing these intervals on on the low or high E strings on your guitar and listen to the difference in sounds:

Intervals on 1 String

1. Open String then 1st Fret = Minor 2nd:

2. Open String then 2nd Fret = Major 2nd:

3. Open String then 3rd Fret = Minor 3rd:

4. Open String then 4th Fret = Major 3rd:

5. Open String then 5th Fret = Perfect 4th:

6. Open String then 6th Fret = Diminished 5th:

7. Open String then 7th Fret = Perfect 5th:

8. Open String then 8th Fret = Minor 6th:

9. Open String then 9th Fret = Major 6th:

10. Open String then 10 Fret = Minor 7th:

11. Open String then 11th Fret = Major 7th:

12. Open String then 12th Fret = Octave:

Lesson 2: C Major Triad: Root Position: 6th String, 8th Fret

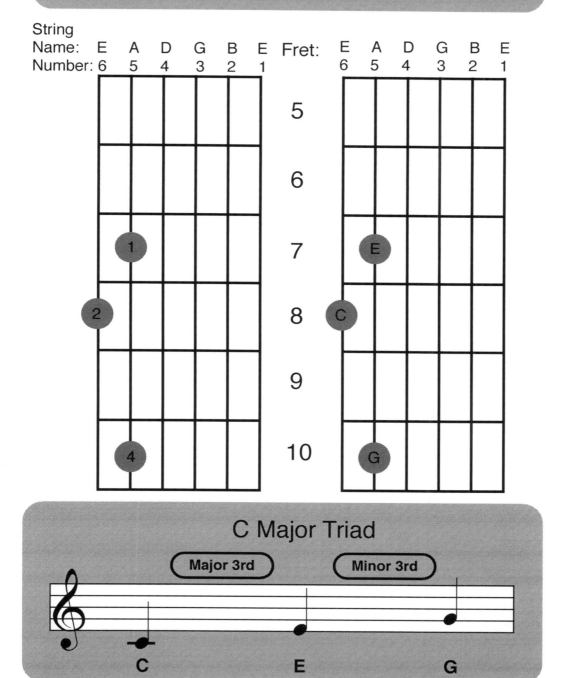

Lesson 3: C Major Triad: Root Position: 5th String, 3rd Fret

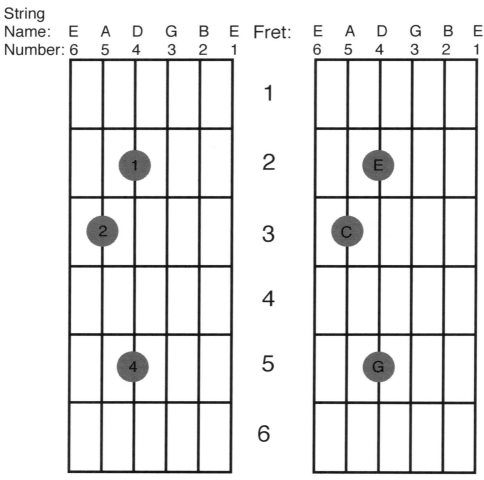

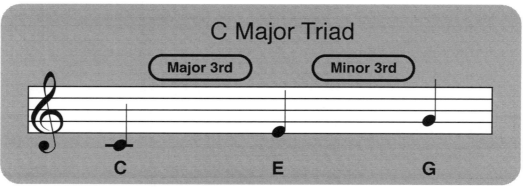

C Major Triad

Major 3rd   Minor 3rd

C   E   G

Lesson 4: C Major Triad: Root Position: 4th String, 10th Fret

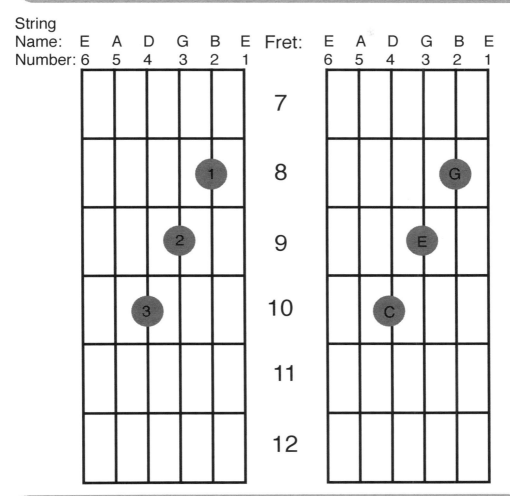

C Major Triad

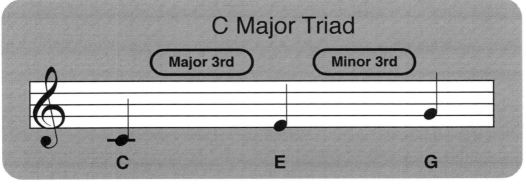

Lesson 5: C Major Triad: Root Position: 3rd String, 5th Fret

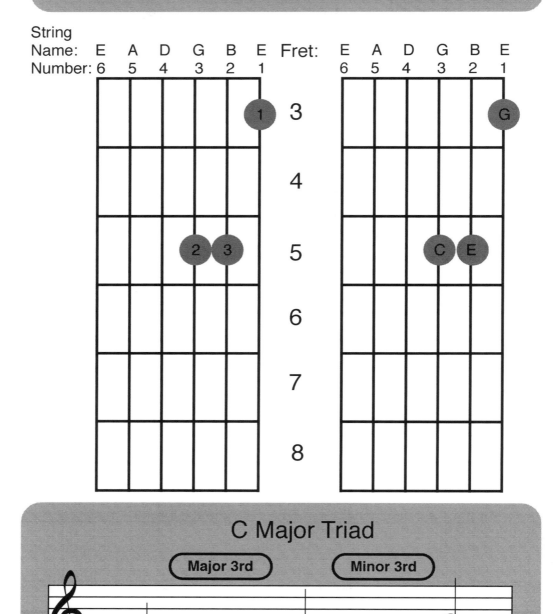

String
Name: E   A   D   G   B   E   Fret: E   A   D   G   B   E
Number: 6   5   4   3   2   1   6   5   4   3   2   1

C Major Triad

Major 3rd   Minor 3rd

C   E   G

Lesson 6: C Major Triad: Root Position: 2nd String, 13th Fret

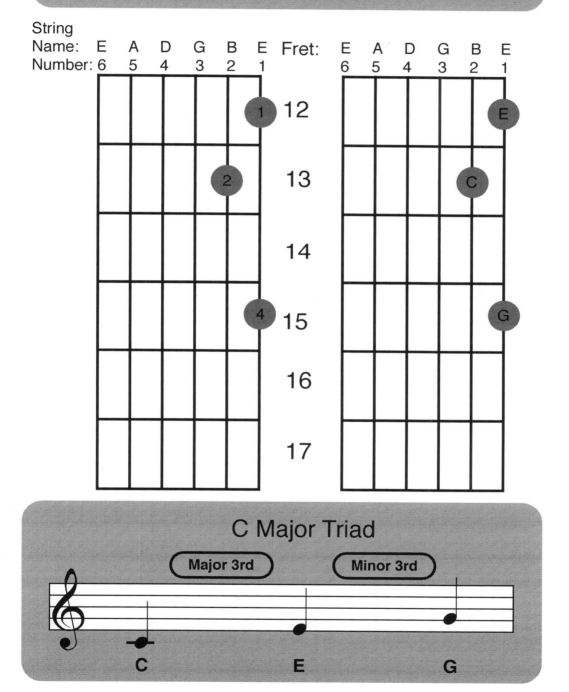

String
Name: E A D G B E   Fret: E A D G B E
Number: 6 5 4 3 2 1   6 5 4 3 2 1

C Major Triad

Major 3rd   Minor 3rd

C   E   G

Lesson 7: Major Arpeggios: Overview & Play-Along Video

- Major Arpeggios (also called "Major Triads") are composed of 3 notes: The Root, the Third, and the Fifth. In a C Major Arpeggio, the Root is C, the Third is E, and the Fifth is G.

- The Root is the most important note of the arpeggio. For example the Root of a G Major Arpeggio is "G"; the Root of an E Major Arpeggio is "E".

- In all Major Arpeggios the distance between the Root and the Third of the Arpeggio is a Major 3rd Interval.

- In all Major Arpeggios the distance between the Third and the Fifth of the arpeggio is a Minor 3rd Interval.

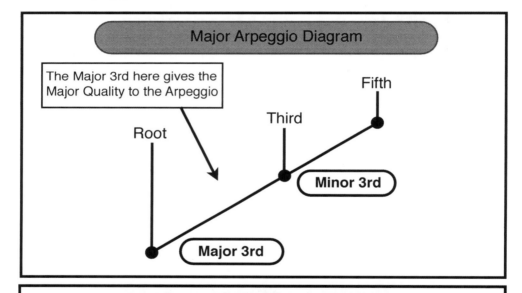

Major Arpeggio Diagram

The Major 3rd here gives the Major Quality to the Arpeggio

Fifth

Third

Root

Minor 3rd

Major 3rd

Play-Along Video 1

- For Play-Along Video #1, try playing the different finger patterns for the C Major Triad Arpeggios over the chords on the video.

- Type "GuitarArpeggioHandbook" (all one word) into the Youtube search field.

Lesson 8: A Minor Triad: Root Position: 6th String, 5th Fret

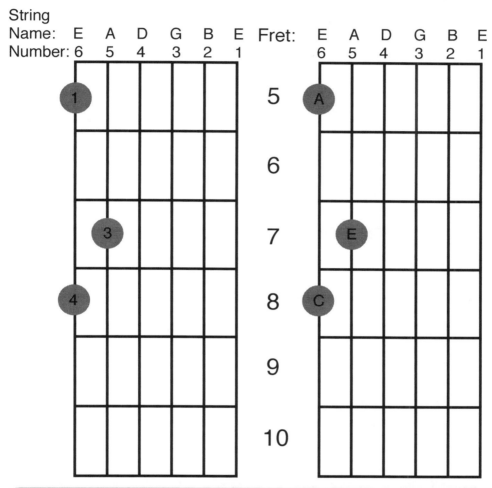

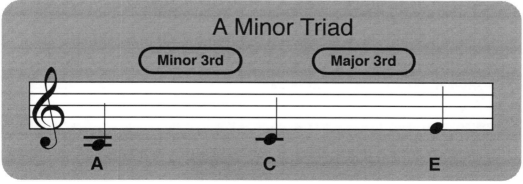

A Minor Triad

Minor 3rd   Major 3rd

A   C   E

Lesson 9: A Minor Triad: Root Position: 5th String, 12th Fret

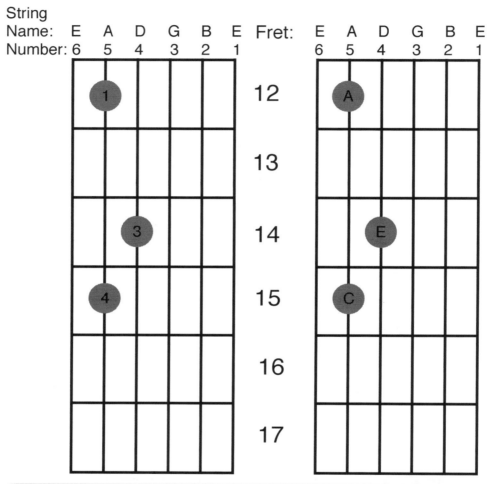

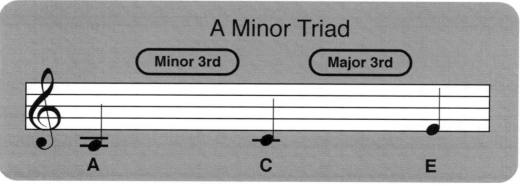

A Minor Triad

Minor 3rd   Major 3rd

A   C   E

Lesson 10: A Minor Triad: Root Position: 4th String, 7th Fret

String Name:	E	A	D	G	B	E	Fret:	E	A	D	G	B	E
Number:	6	5	4	3	2	1		6	5	4	3	2	1

Left diagram (fret 5): G string (3) = 1, B string (2) = 2; fret 7: D string (4) = 4

Right diagram (fret 5): G string (3) = C, B string (2) = E; fret 7: D string (4) = A

Fret markers: 5, 6, 7, 8, 9, 10

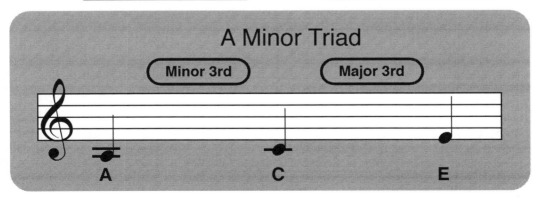

A Minor Triad

Minor 3rd   Major 3rd

A   C   E

Lesson 11: A Minor Triad: Root Position: 3rd String, 14th Fret

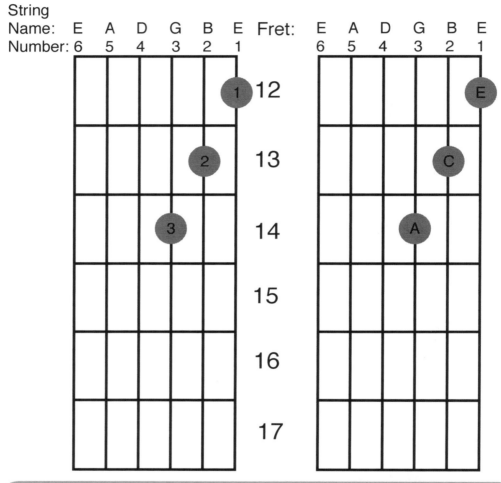

String Name: E A D G B E Fret: E A D G B E
Number: 6 5 4 3 2 1 6 5 4 3 2 1

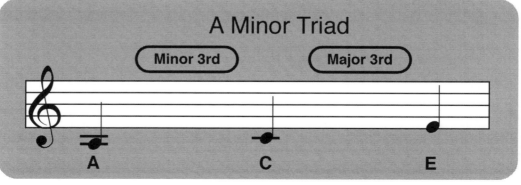

A Minor Triad

Minor 3rd   Major 3rd

A   C   E

Lesson 12: A Minor Triad: Root Position: 2nd String, 10th Fret

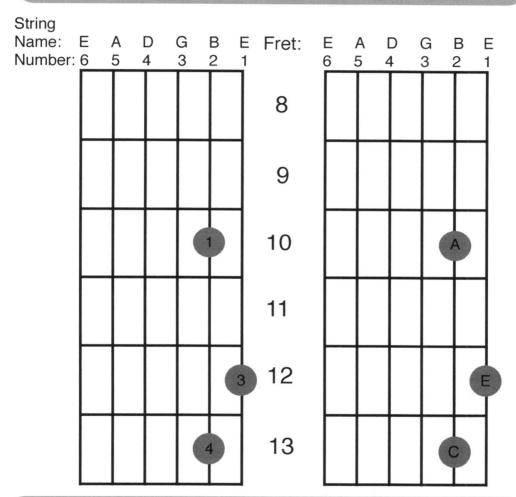

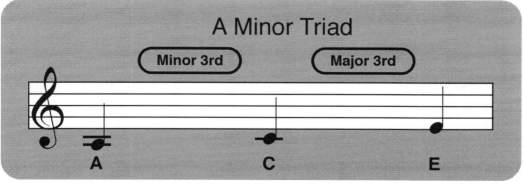

A Minor Triad

Minor 3rd   Major 3rd

A   C   E

Lesson 13: Minor Arpeggios: Overview & Play-Along Video

- Minor Arpeggios (also called "Minor Triads") are composed of 3 notes: The Root, the Third, and the Fifth. In a C Minor Arpeggio, the Root is C, the Third is E Flat, and the Fifth is G.

- The Root is the most important note of the arpeggio. For example the Root of a G Minor Arpeggio is "G"; the Root of an E Minor Arpeggio is "E".

- In all Minor arpeggios the distance between the Root and the Third of the arpeggio is a Minor 3rd Interval. This Minor Third interval between the Root and Third gives the arpeggio its defining characteristic.

- In all Minor Arpeggios the distance between the Third and the Fifth of the arpeggios is a Major 3rd Interval.

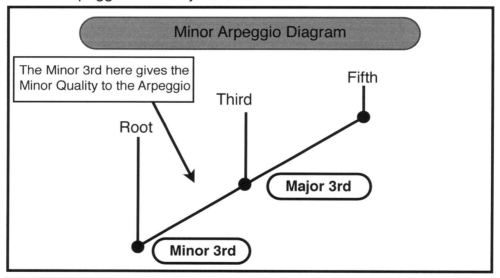

Minor Arpeggio Diagram

The Minor 3rd here gives the Minor Quality to the Arpeggio

Fifth

Third

Root

Major 3rd

Minor 3rd

Play-Along Video 2

- For Play-Along Video #2, try playing the different finger patterns for the A Minor Triad Arpeggios.

- Type "GuitarArpeggioHandbook" (all one word) into the Youtube search field.

Lesson 14: Music Theory Overview: Diminished & Augmented Arpeggios

- Diminished Arpeggios are Triads where the distances between the Root and Third and the Third and Fifth of the Arpeggio are both Minor Third Intervals.

- Augmented Arpeggios are Triads where the distances between the Root and Third and the Third and Fifth of the Arpeggio are both Major Third Intervals.

- Diminished and Augmented Arpeggios have a tense and energized quality. They work very well as transitions between Major and Minor Arpeggios. Check out *Guitar Adventures 2* for some great Diminished and Augmented Arpeggio Licks!

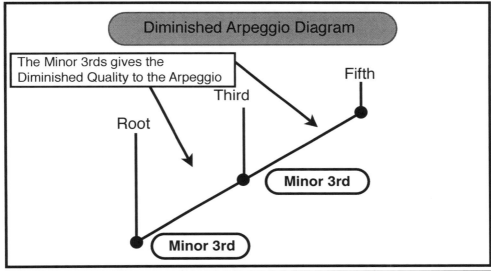

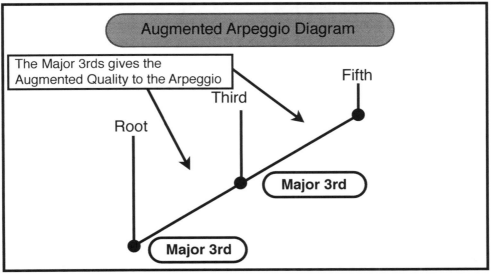

Lesson 15: D Diminished Triad: Root Position: 6th String, 10th Fret

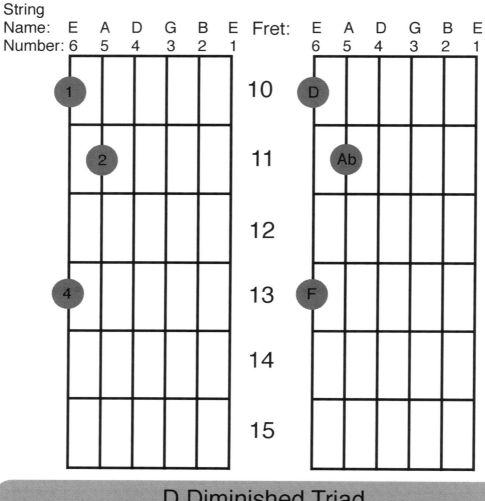

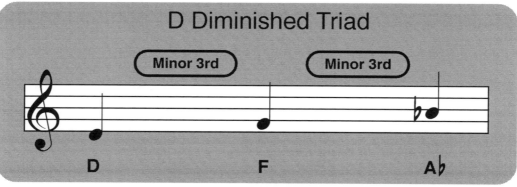

D Diminished Triad

Minor 3rd   Minor 3rd

D   F   Ab

Lesson 16: D Diminished Triad: Root Position: 5th String, 5th Fret

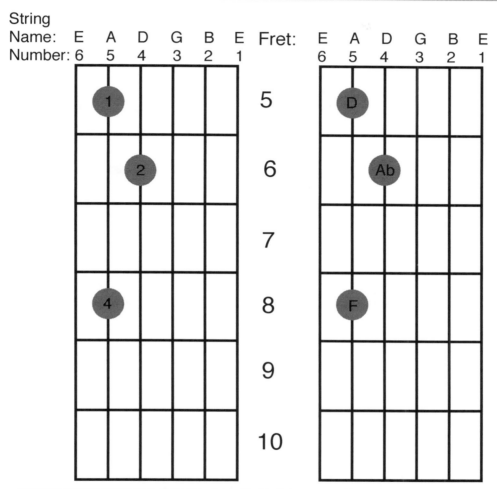

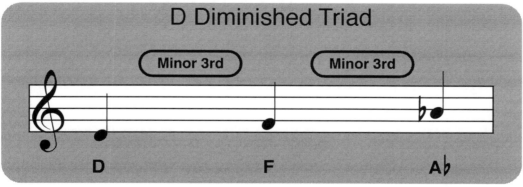

D Diminished Triad

Minor 3rd   Minor 3rd

D   F   Ab

Lesson 17: D Diminished Triad: Root Position: 4th String, 12th Fret

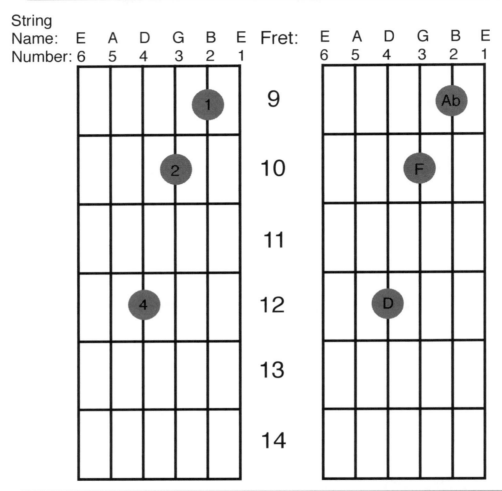

D Diminished Triad

Lesson 18: D Diminished Triad: Root Position: 3rd String, 7th Fret

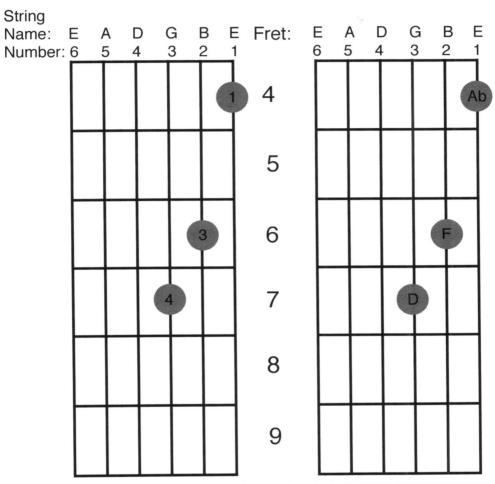

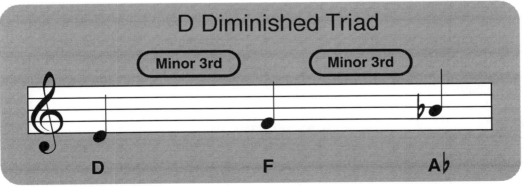

D Diminished Triad

Minor 3rd   Minor 3rd

D   F   Ab

Lesson 19: D Diminished Triad: Root Position: 2nd String, 3rd Fret

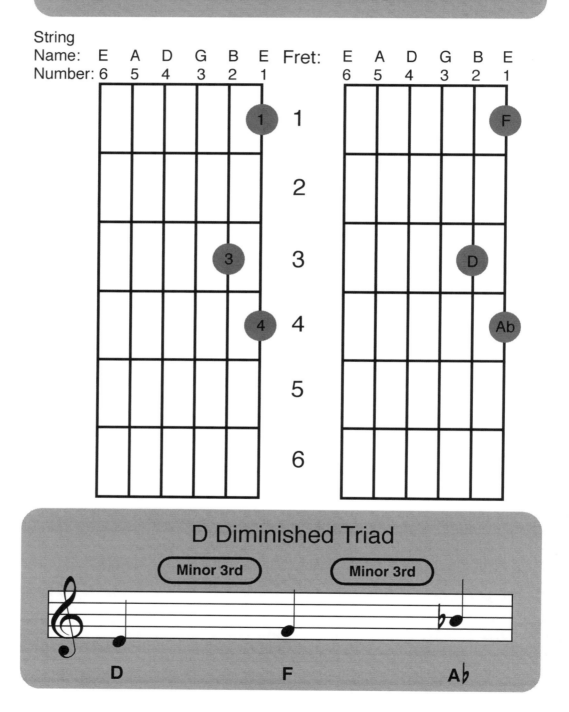

String Name: E A D G B E
Number: 6 5 4 3 2 1

Fret:

E A D G B E
6 5 4 3 2 1

D Diminished Triad

Minor 3rd   Minor 3rd

D   F   Ab

Lesson 20: C Augmented Triad: Root Position: 6th String, 8th Fret

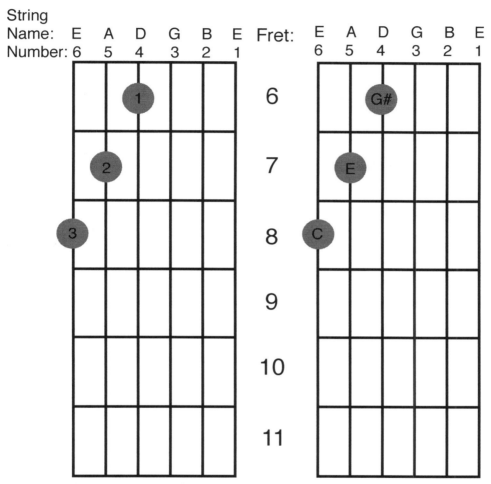

String
Name: E A D G B E   Fret: E A D G B E
Number: 6 5 4 3 2 1   6 5 4 3 2 1

C Augmented Triad

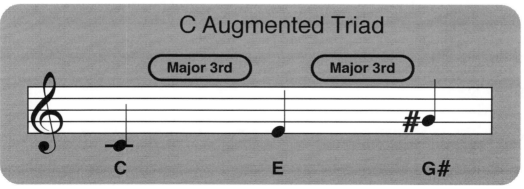

Major 3rd   Major 3rd

C   E   G#

Lesson 21: C Augmented Triad: Root Position: 5th String, 3rd Fret

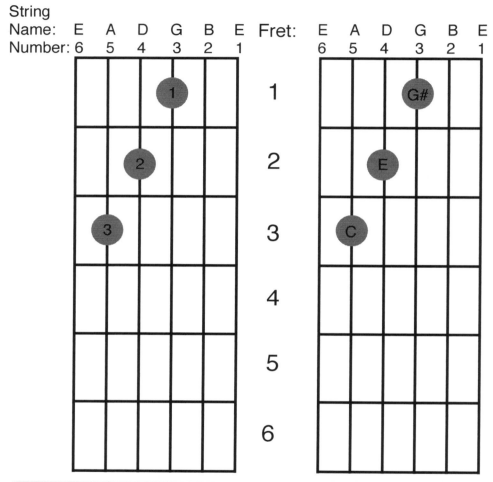

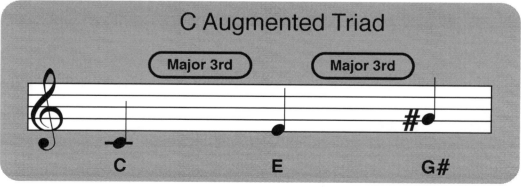

C Augmented Triad

Major 3rd   Major 3rd

C   E   G#

Lesson 22: C Augmented Triad: Root Position: 4th String, 10th Fret

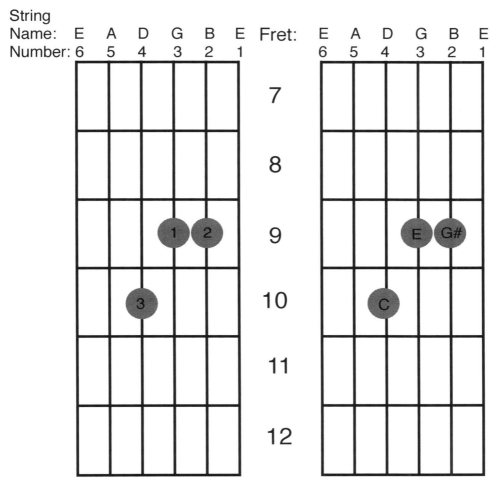

String Name:	E	A	D	G	B	E	Fret:	E	A	D	G	B	E
Number:	6	5	4	3	2	1		6	5	4	3	2	1

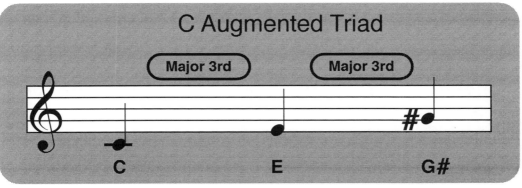

C Augmented Triad

Major 3rd   Major 3rd

C   E   G#

Lesson 23: C Augmented Triad: Root Position: 3rd String, 5th Fret

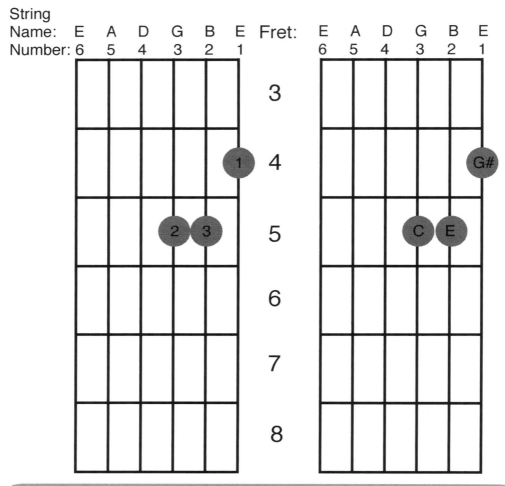

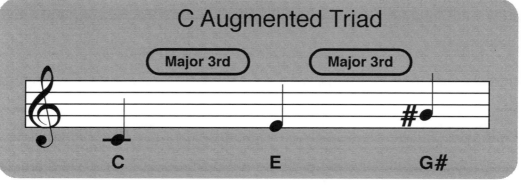

C Augmented Triad

Lesson 24: C Augmented Triad: Root Position: 2nd String, 13th Fret

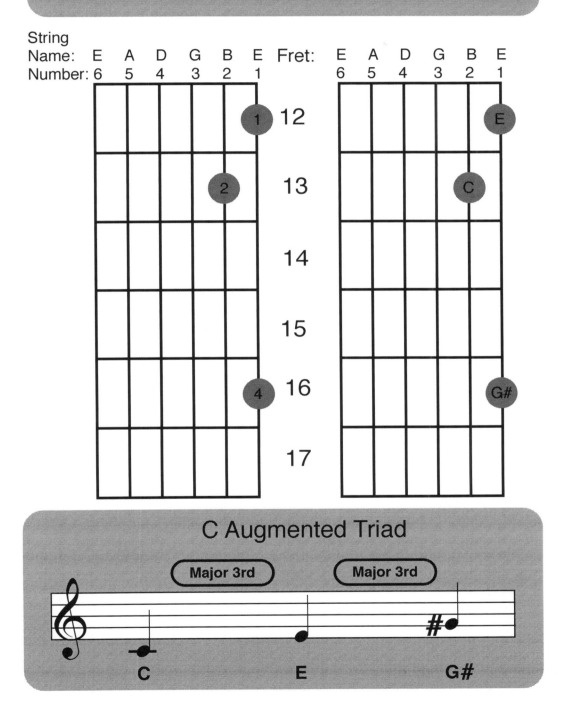

C Augmented Triad

Lesson 25: Inversions: Music Theory Overview

- An Inversion is an Arpeggio or Chord where the lowest note is not the root of the Arpeggio or Chord. For example, the First Inversion of a C Major Arpeggio is "E", "G", and "C" (see example below).

- All Arpeggios and Chords have Inversions. The term inversion just means mixing up the order of the notes in an Arpeggio or Chord.

- If an Arpeggio has 3 notes, for example C Major ("C", "E", and "G"), it has 2 inversions: 1st Inversion and 2nd Inversion. If an Arpeggio has 4 notes, for example C Major 7th ("C", "E", "G", and "B") it has 3 inversions: 1st Inversion, 2nd Inversion, and 3rd Inversion.

- Playing Inversions of Chords and Arpeggios adds a lot of variety, power, and excitement to your songs and guitar solos. Check out *Guitar Adventures 1 & 2* for lessons on how to add inversions and new techniques to your chord playing.

Inversions for C Major

- In the following pages, you will be learning inversions for Major and Minor Arpeggios.

- As you practice these new forms, listen to the difference in sound between the Root Position, 1st Inversion, and 2nd Inversion Forms.

- These Inversions will help you create greater nuance and expression in your playing.

Here is a C Major Chord in Root Position or "Root Form":

C is the Root
E is the 3rd
G is the 5th

Here is a C Major Chord in 1st Inversion or "1st Form"

Here is a C Major Chord in 2nd Inversion or "2nd Form"

Lesson 26: C Major Triad: 1st Inversion: 6th String, 12th Fret

String
Name:
Number:

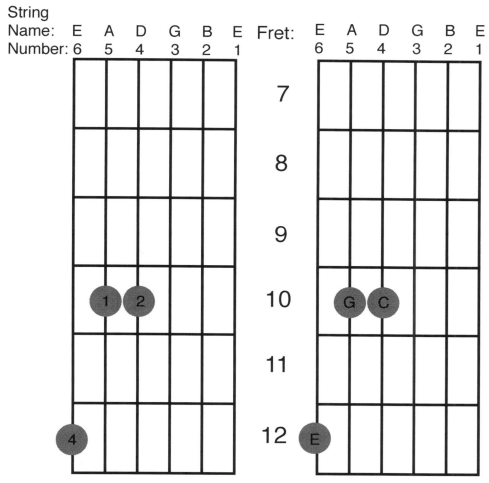

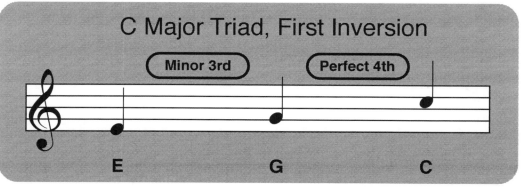

C Major Triad, First Inversion

Minor 3rd   Perfect 4th

E   G   C

Lesson 27: C Major Triad: 1st Inversion: 5th String, 7th Fret

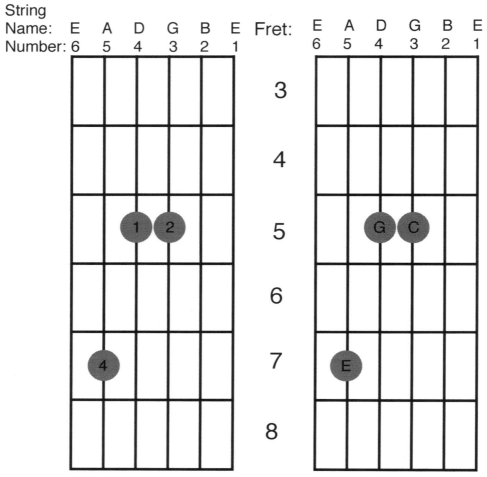

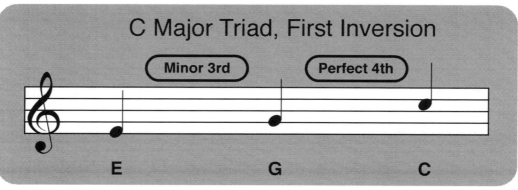

C Major Triad, First Inversion

Minor 3rd   Perfect 4th

E   G   C

Lesson 28: C Major Triad: 1st Inversion: 4th String, 14th Fret

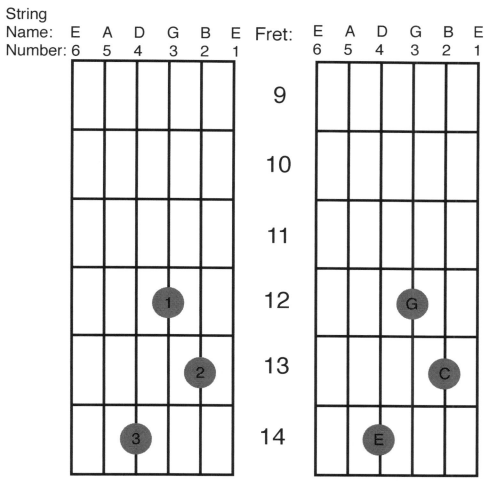

C Major Triad, First Inversion

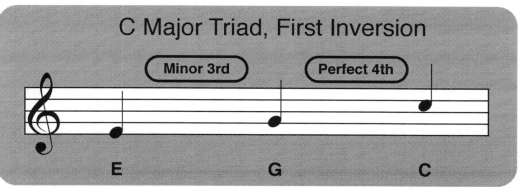

Minor 3rd   Perfect 4th

E   G   C

Lesson 29: C Major Triad: 1st Inversion: 3rd String, 9th Fret

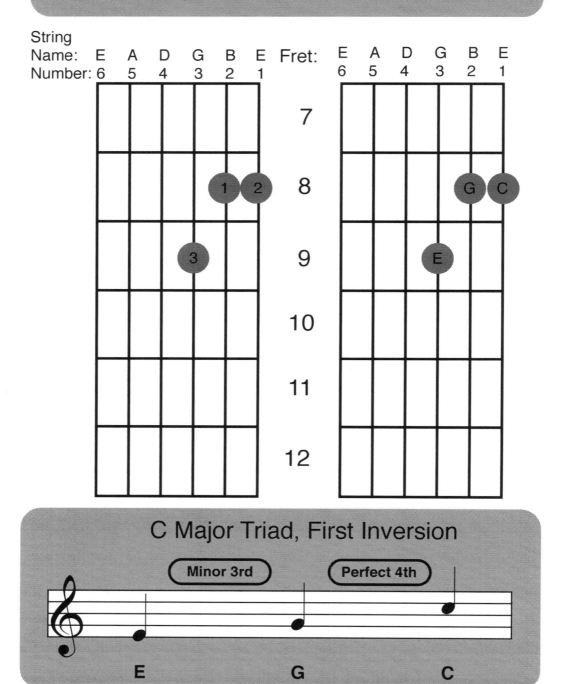

C Major Triad, First Inversion

Lesson 30: C Major Triad: 1st Inversion: 2nd String, 5th Fret

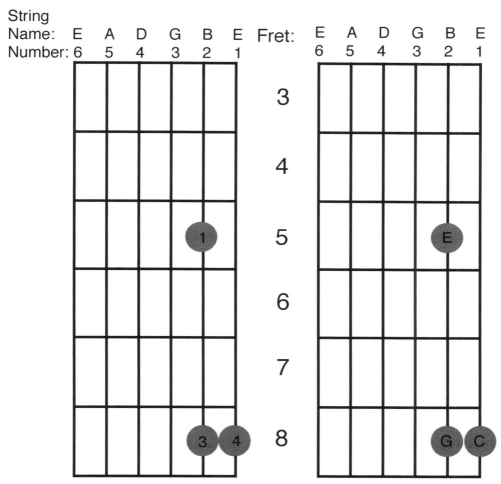

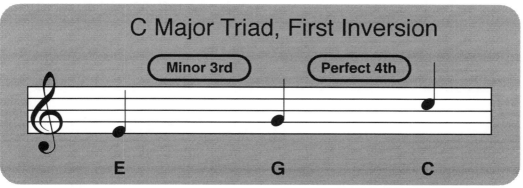

C Major Triad, First Inversion

Minor 3rd   Perfect 4th

E   G   C

Lesson 31: A Minor Triad: 1st Inversion: 6th String, 8th Fret

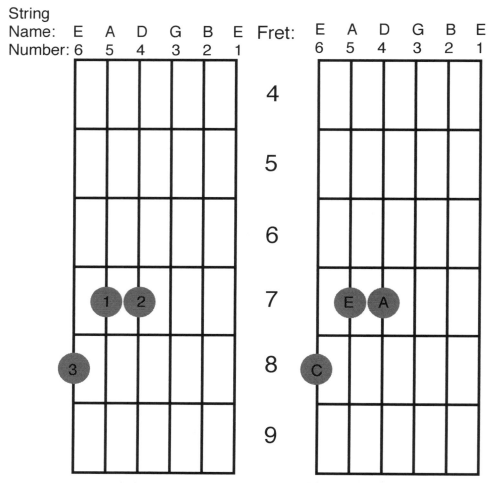

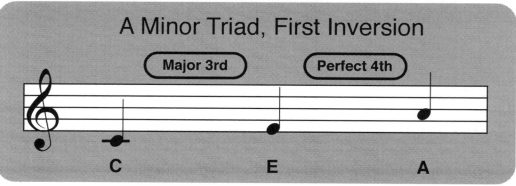

A Minor Triad, First Inversion

Major 3rd   Perfect 4th

C   E   A

Lesson 32: A Minor Triad: 1st Inversion: 5th String, 3rd Fret

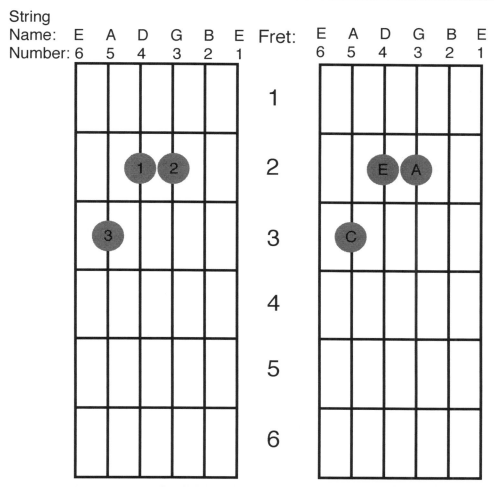

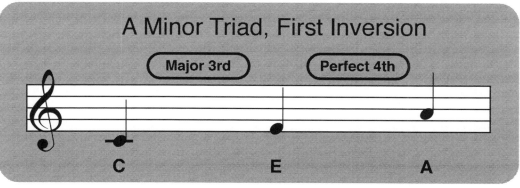

A Minor Triad, First Inversion

Major 3rd   Perfect 4th

C   E   A

Lesson 33: A Minor Triad: 1st Inversion: 4th String, 10th Fret

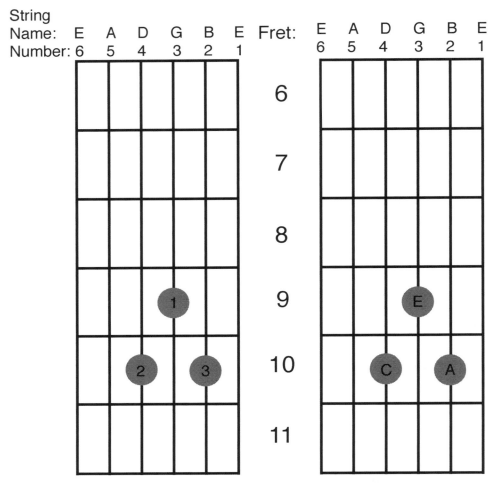

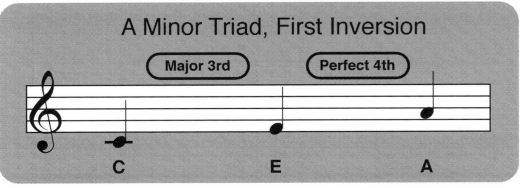

A Minor Triad, First Inversion

Lesson 34: A Minor Triad: 1st Inversion: 3rd String, 5th Fret

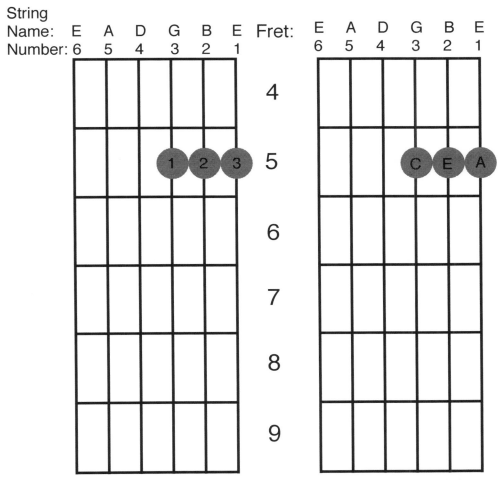

A Minor Triad, First Inversion

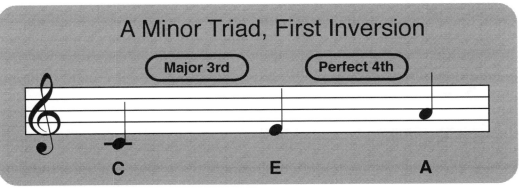

Lesson 35: A Minor Triad: 1st Inversion: 2nd String, 1st Fret

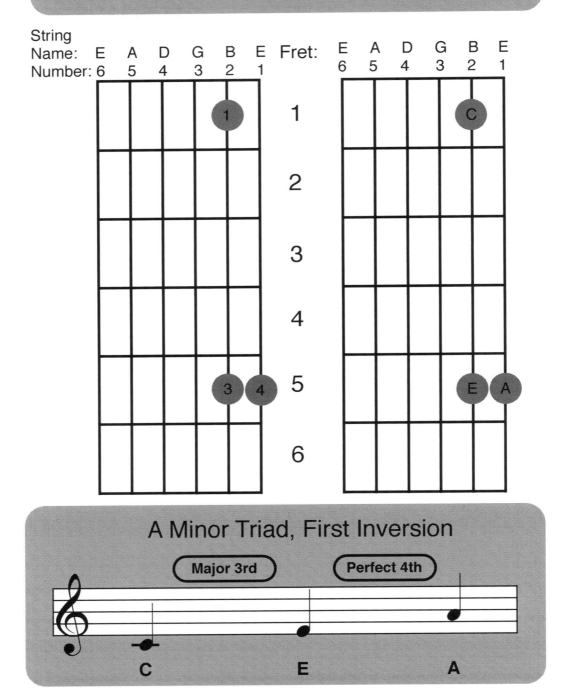

A Minor Triad, First Inversion

Major 3rd   Perfect 4th

C   E   A

Lesson 36: C Major Triad: 2nd Inversion: 6th String, 3rd Fret

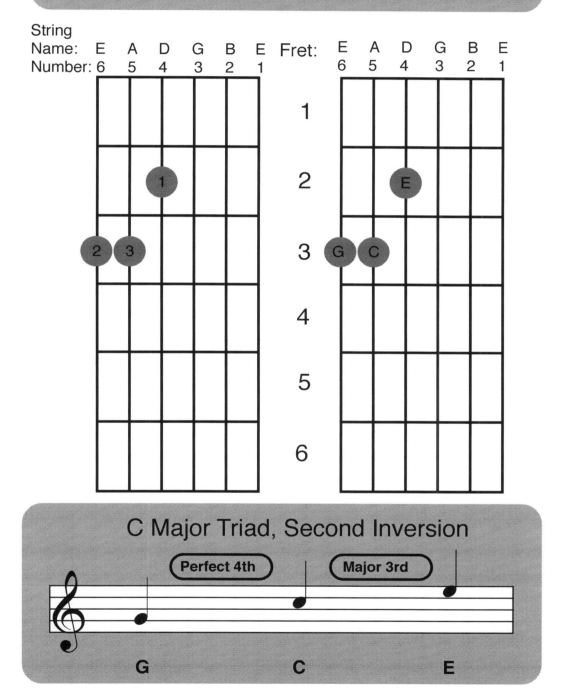

C Major Triad, Second Inversion

Lesson 37: C Major Triad: 2nd Inversion: 5th String, 8th Fret

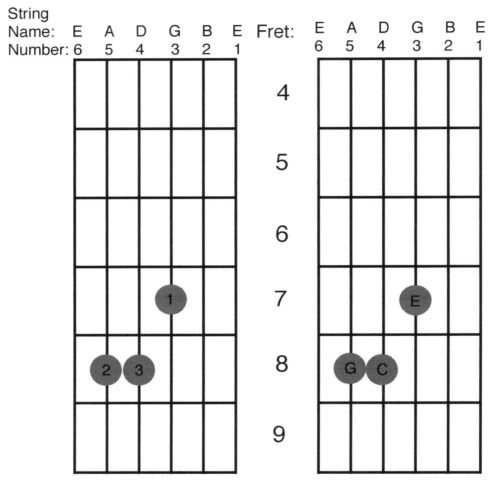

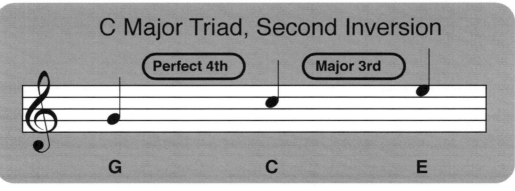

C Major Triad, Second Inversion

Lesson 38: C Major Triad: 2nd Inversion: 4th String, 5th Fret

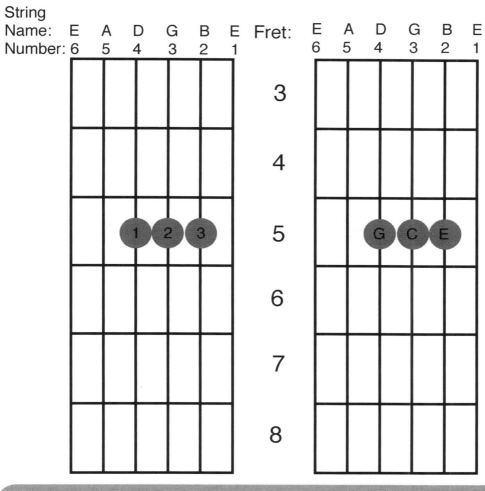

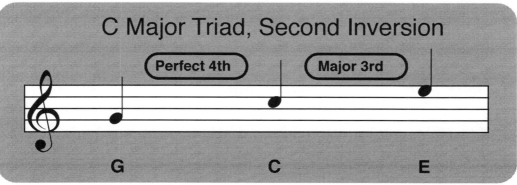

C Major Triad, Second Inversion

Lesson 39: C Major Triad: 2nd Inversion: 3rd String, 12th Fret

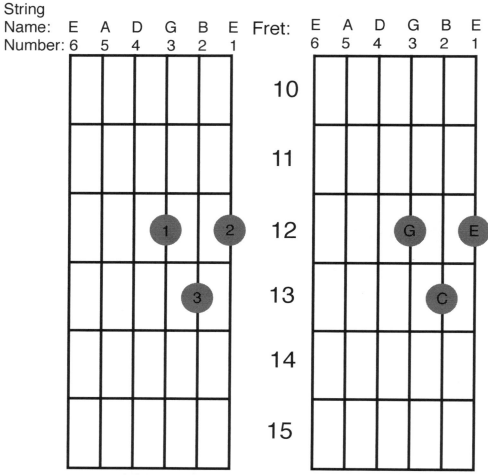

String Name: E A D G B E   Fret: E A D G B E
Number: 6 5 4 3 2 1   6 5 4 3 2 1

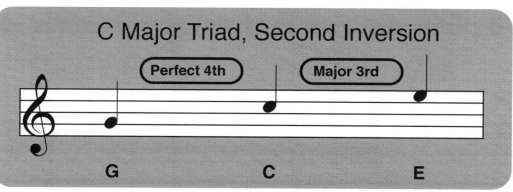

C Major Triad, Second Inversion

Perfect 4th   Major 3rd

G   C   E

Lesson 40: C Major Triad: 2nd Inversion: 2nd String, 8th Fret

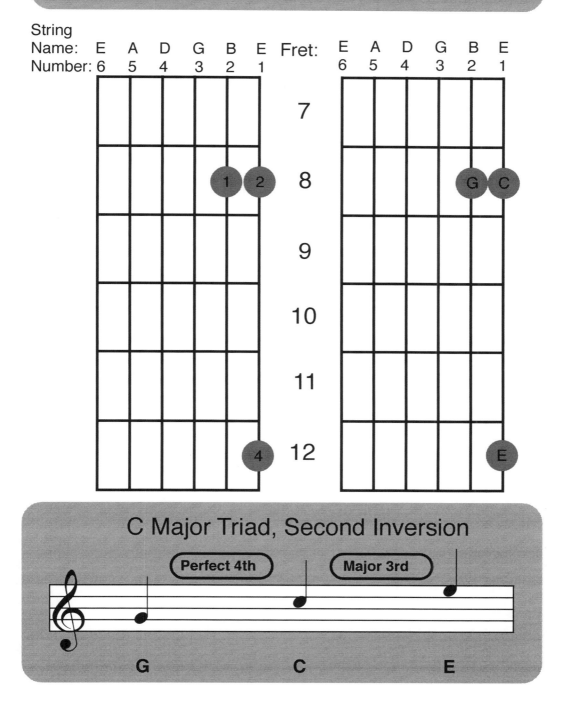

C Major Triad, Second Inversion

Perfect 4th   Major 3rd

G   C   E

Lesson 41: A Minor Triad: 2nd Inversion: 6th String, 12th Fret

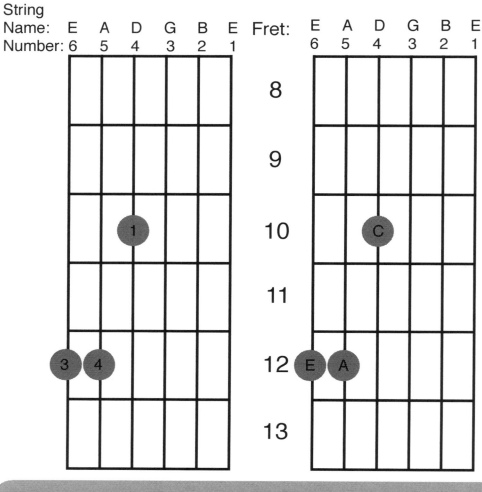

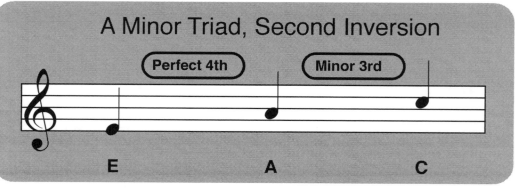

A Minor Triad, Second Inversion

Perfect 4th   Minor 3rd

E   A   C

Lesson 42: A Minor Triad: 2nd Inversion: 5th String, 7th Fret

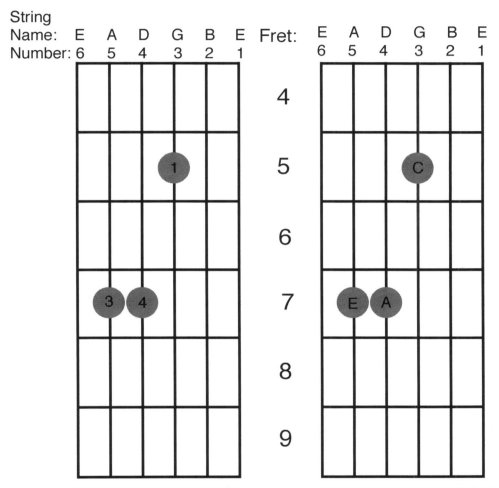

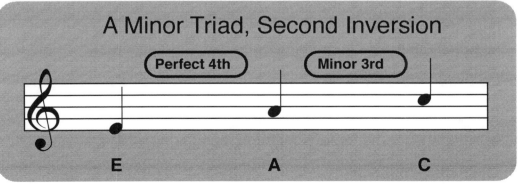

A Minor Triad, Second Inversion

Perfect 4th   Minor 3rd

E   A   C

Lesson 43: A Minor Triad: 2nd Inversion: 4th String, 2nd Fret

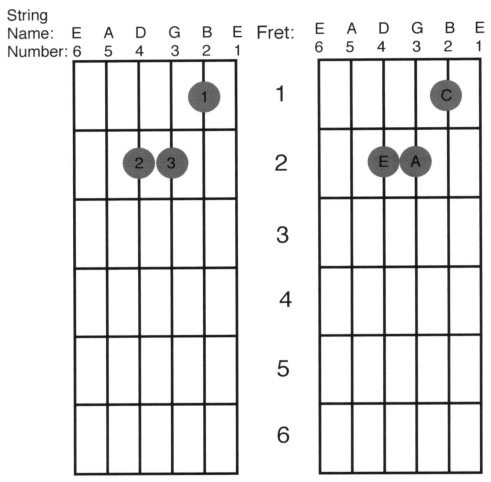

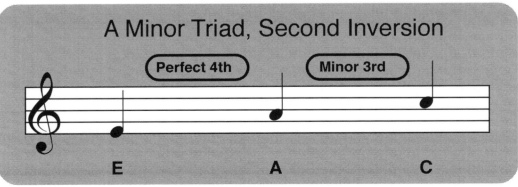

A Minor Triad, Second Inversion

Lesson 44: A Minor Triad: 2nd Inversion: 3rd String, 9th Fret

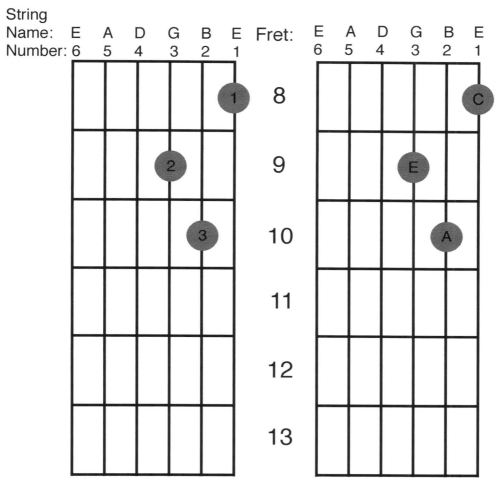

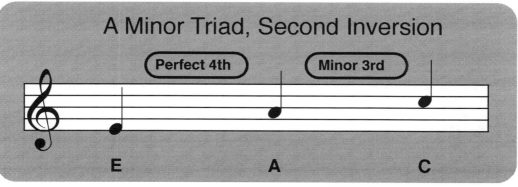

A Minor Triad, Second Inversion

Lesson 45: A Minor Triad: 2nd Inversion: 2nd String, 5th Fret

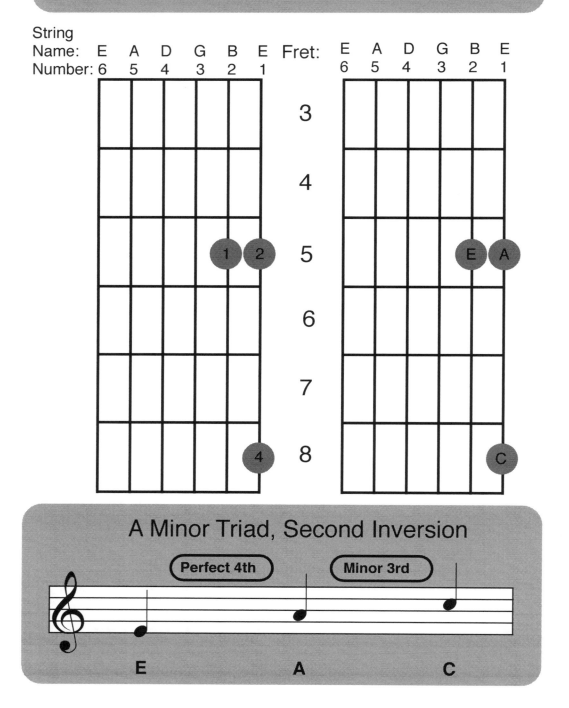

A Minor Triad, Second Inversion

Lesson 46: Arpeggio Technique & Play-Along Video in C Major & A Minor

- A number of arpeggios, especially ones played on 2 strings, involve wide stretches for the left hand. In order to play these arpeggios fluidly, bring the thumb of the left hand down behind the guitar neck. It is best if the thumb is roughly parallel to the first finger. This will increase the span for the left-hand fingers.

- Try playing the inversions for C Major Arpeggios and A Minor Arpeggios over Play-Along Video 3 and listen to how they sound over the chord changes.

- Type "GuitarArpeggioHandbook" (all one word) into Youtube.

Play-Along Video 3

C	C	Am	Am
C	C	Am	Am
C	C	Am	Am

Section

2

4-Note Arpeggios

Lesson 47: D Major Triad: Root Position: 6th String, 10th Fret

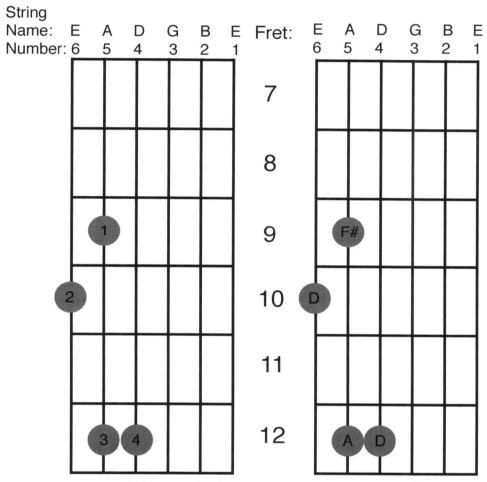

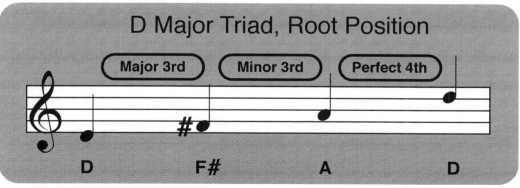

D Major Triad, Root Position

Major 3rd   Minor 3rd   Perfect 4th

D   F#   A   D

Lesson 48: D Major Triad: Root Position: 5th String, 5th Fret

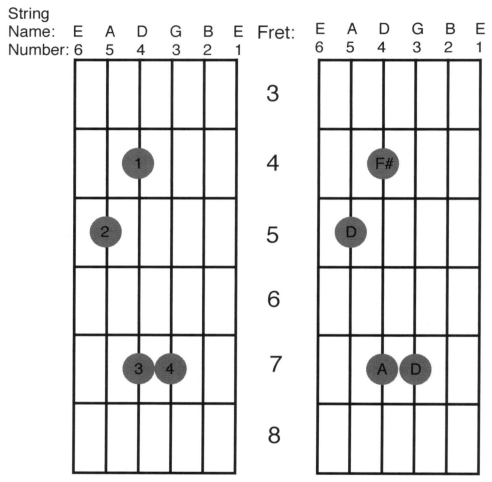

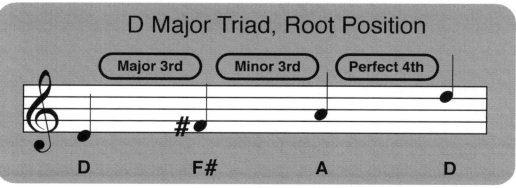

D Major Triad, Root Position

Major 3rd   Minor 3rd   Perfect 4th

D   F#   A   D

Lesson 49: D Major Triad: Root Position: 4th String, 12th Fret

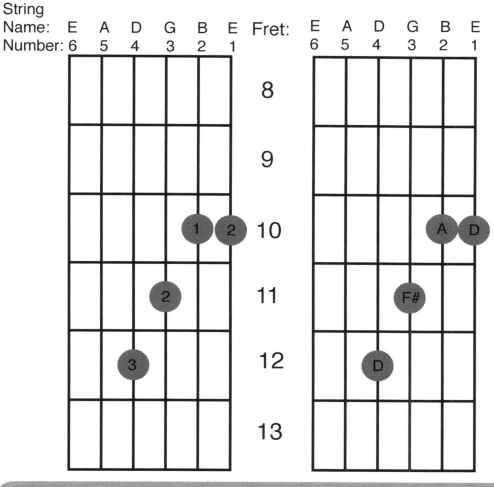

String
Name: E A D G B E   Fret: E A D G B E
Number: 6 5 4 3 2 1   6 5 4 3 2 1

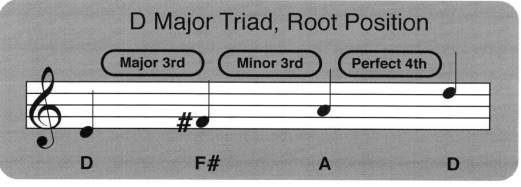

D Major Triad, Root Position

Major 3rd   Minor 3rd   Perfect 4th

D   F#   A   D

Lesson 50: D Major Triad: Root Position: 3rd String, 7th Fret

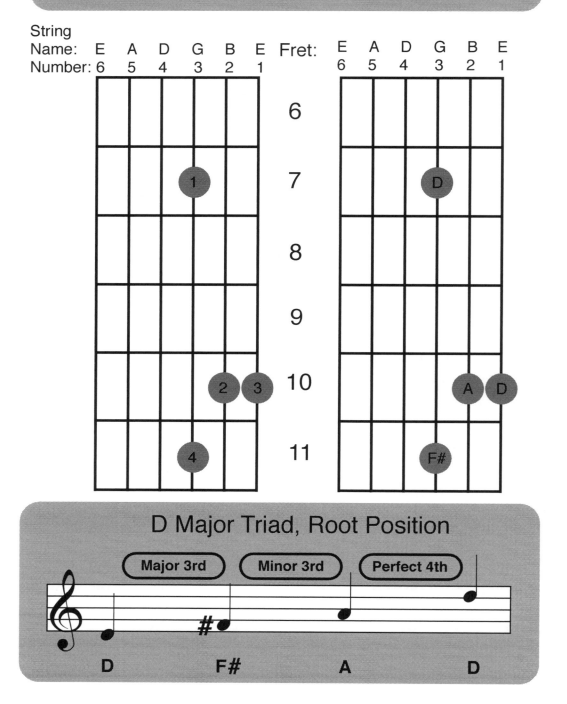

String Name: E A D G B E Fret: E A D G B E
Number: 6 5 4 3 2 1 6 5 4 3 2 1

D Major Triad, Root Position

Major 3rd   Minor 3rd   Perfect 4th

D   F#   A   D

Lesson 51: D Major Triad: Root Position: 2nd String, 3rd Fret

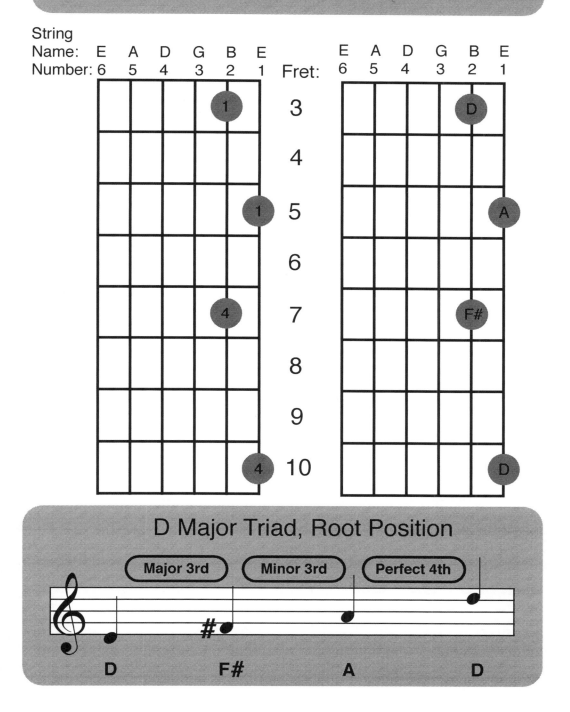

Lesson 52: D Minor Triad: Root Position: 6th String, 10th Fret

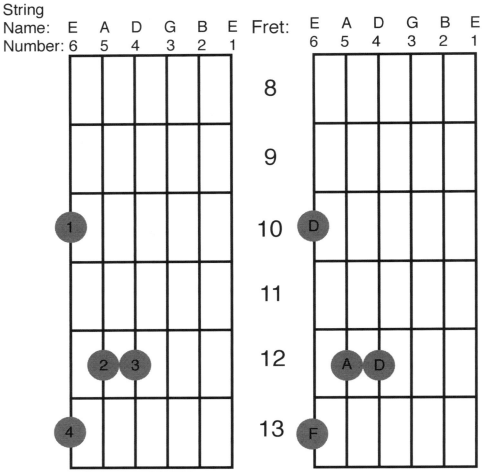

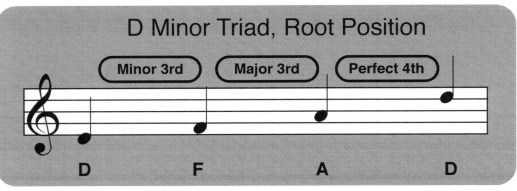

D Minor Triad, Root Position

Lesson 53: D Minor Triad: Root Position: 5th String, 5th Fret

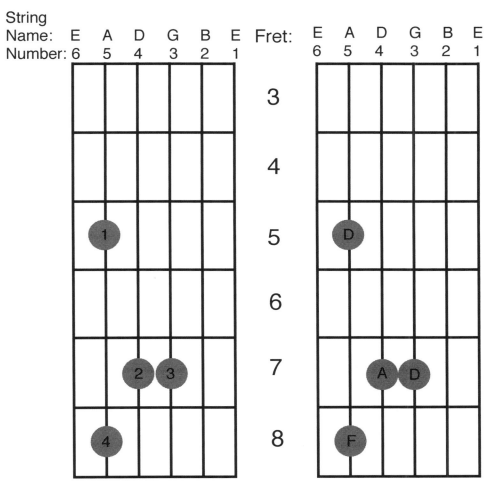

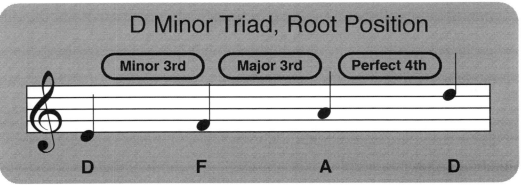

D Minor Triad, Root Position

Minor 3rd   Major 3rd   Perfect 4th

D   F   A   D

Lesson 54: D Minor Triad: Root Position: 4th String, 12th Fret

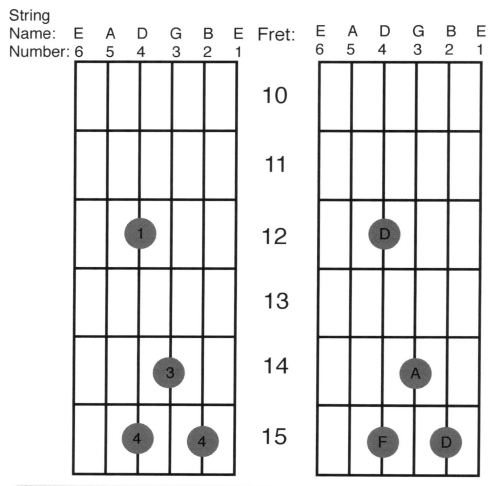

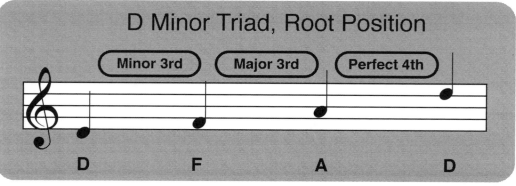

D Minor Triad, Root Position

Minor 3rd   Major 3rd   Perfect 4th

D   F   A   D

Lesson 55: D Minor Triad: Root Position: 3rd String, 7th Fret

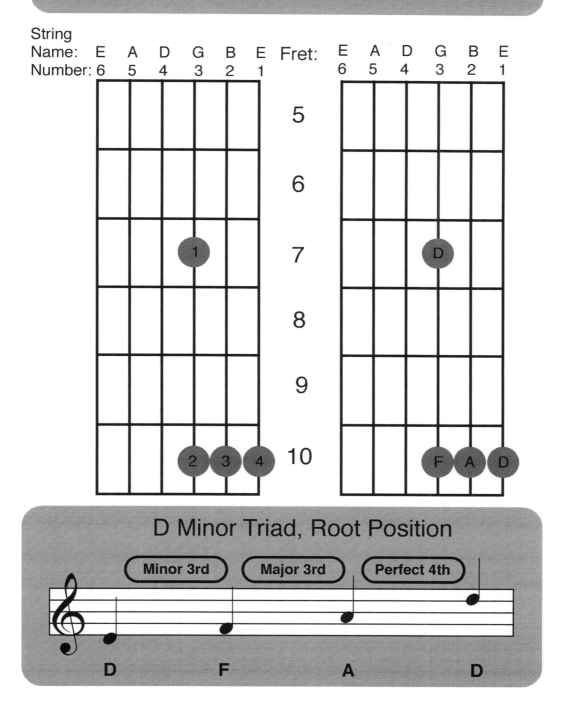

D Minor Triad, Root Position

Lesson 56: D Minor Triad: Root Position: 2nd String, 3rd Fret

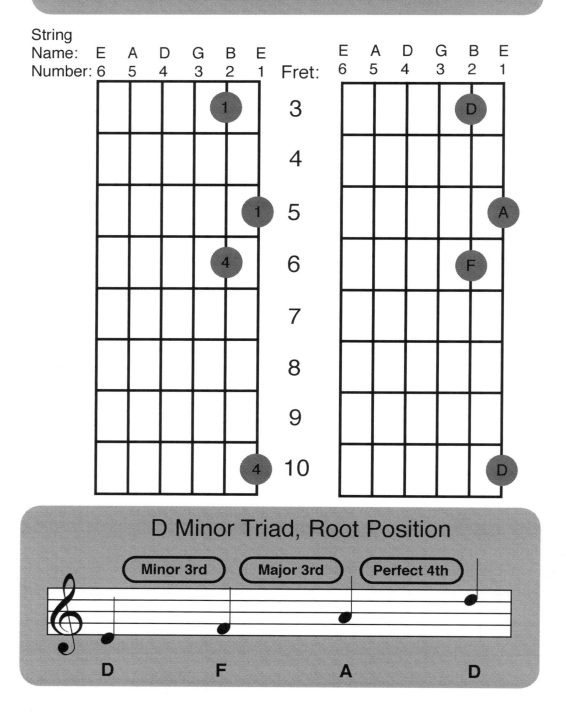

D Minor Triad, Root Position

Minor 3rd Major 3rd Perfect 4th

D   F   A   D

Lesson 57: D Diminished Triad: Root Position: 6th String, 10th Fret

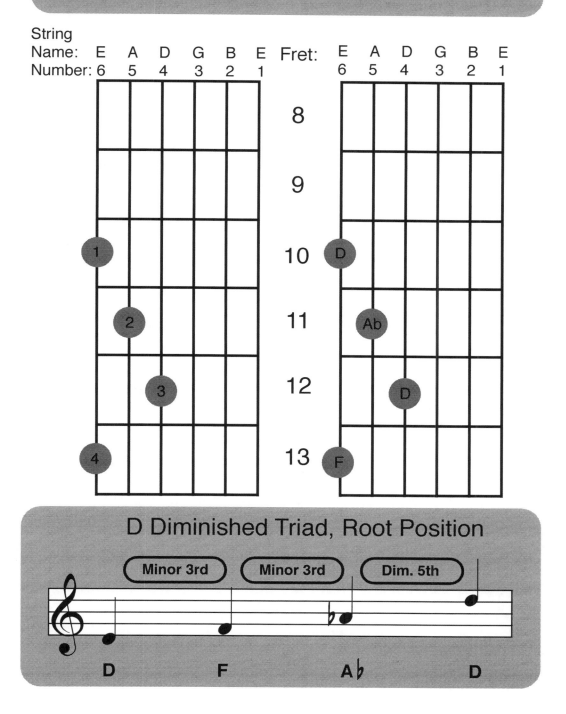

D Diminished Triad, Root Position

Minor 3rd   Minor 3rd   Dim. 5th

D   F   A♭   D

Lesson 58: D Diminished Triad: Root Position: 5th String, 5th Fret

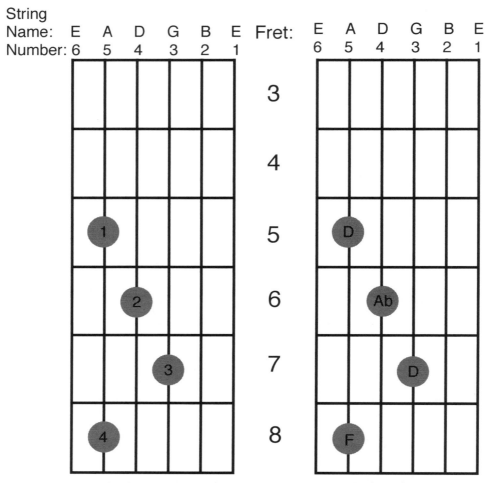

D Diminished Triad, Root Position

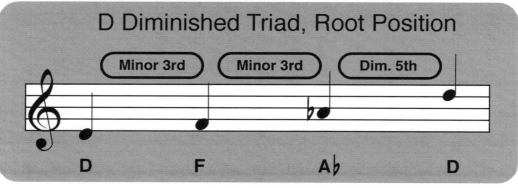

Lesson 59: D Diminished Triad: Root Position: 4th String, 12th Fret

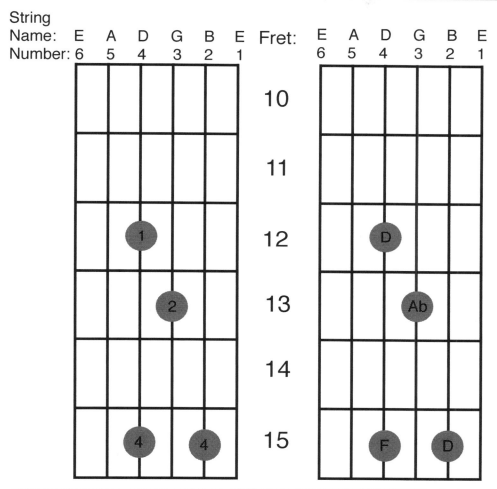

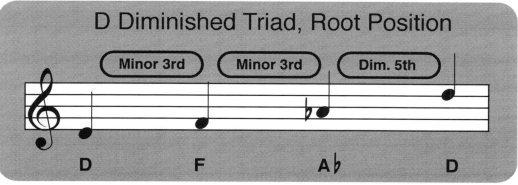

D Diminished Triad, Root Position

Lesson 60: D Diminished Triad: Root Position: 3rd String, 7th Fret

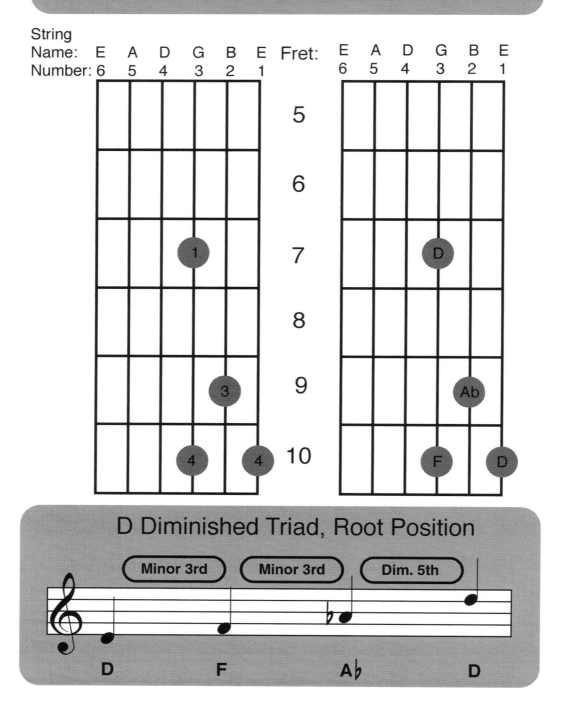

String
Name: E A D G B E   Fret: E A D G B E
Number: 6 5 4 3 2 1   6 5 4 3 2 1

D Diminished Triad, Root Position

Minor 3rd   Minor 3rd   Dim. 5th

D   F   A♭   D

Lesson 61: Arpeggio Technique & Play-Along Video 4: Major, Minor & Diminished Arpeggios

- In order to increase the fluidity of your arpeggio playing, you might try slightly changing the angle of your guitar pick. If you tilt your pick forward or backward between 30 and 45 degrees (depending on which motion is more comfortable for your hand) you will be able to increase the speed of your alternate picking.

- Try playing the D Major, D Minor, and D Diminished Arpeggios over Play-Along Video 4. Listen to the difference in sound between these arpeggios. **Have Fun!**

- Type "GuitarArpeggioHandbook" (all one word) into Youtube.

Play-Along Video 4

D	Dm	Ddim	D
D	Dm	Ddim	D
D	Dm	Ddim	D

Lesson 62: C Augmented Triad: Root Position: 6th String, 8th Fret

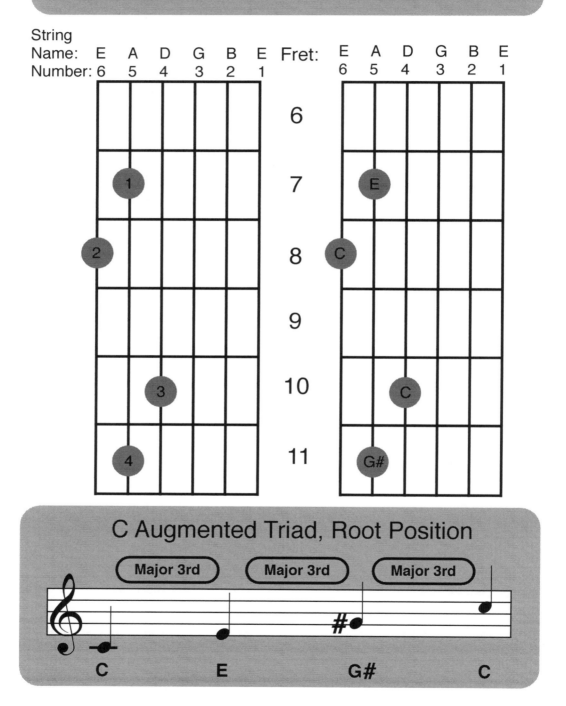

C Augmented Triad, Root Position

Major 3rd   Major 3rd   Major 3rd

C   E   G#   C

Lesson 63: C Augmented Triad: Root Position: 5th String, 3rd Fret

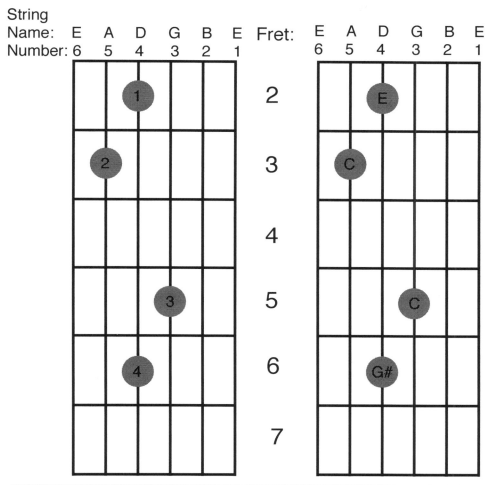

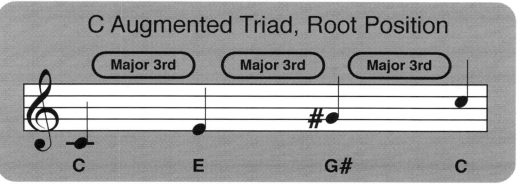

C Augmented Triad, Root Position

Major 3rd   Major 3rd   Major 3rd

C   E   G#   C

Lesson 64: C Augmented Triad: Root Position: 4th String, 10th Fret

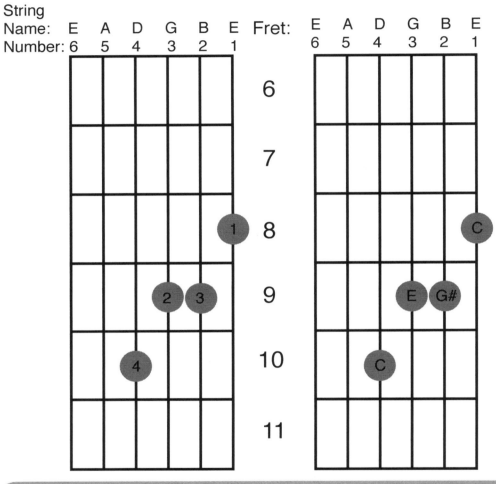

String Name: E A D G B E   Fret: E A D G B E
Number: 6 5 4 3 2 1   6 5 4 3 2 1

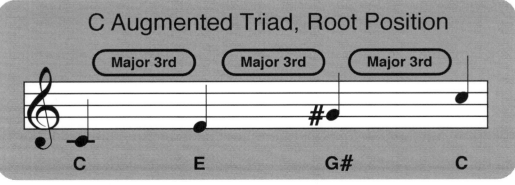

C Augmented Triad, Root Position

Major 3rd   Major 3rd   Major 3rd

C   E   G#   C

Lesson 65: C Augmented Triad: Root Position: 3rd String, 5th Fret

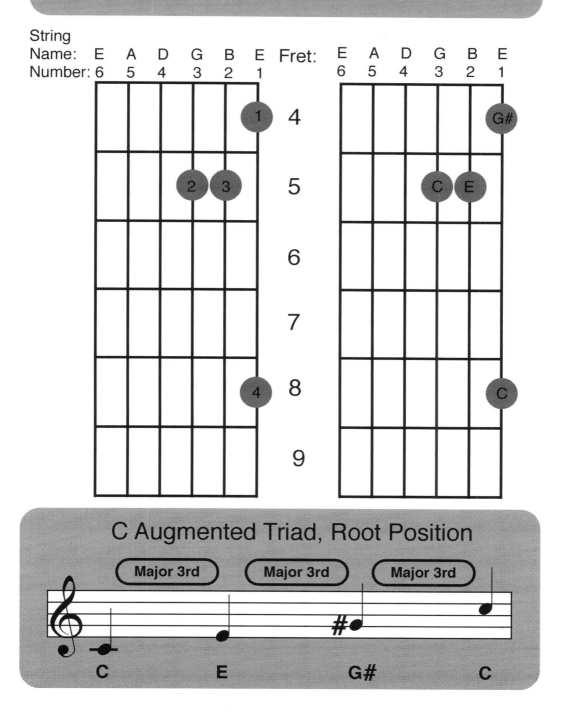

C Augmented Triad, Root Position

Major 3rd   Major 3rd   Major 3rd

C   E   G#   C

Lesson 66: Seventh Arpeggios: Music Theory Overview

- Seventh Arpeggios, for example Dominant 7th, Minor 7th, and Major 7th, all contain 4 notes: A Root, Third, Fifth, and Seventh.

- Dominant 7th Arpeggios contain a Major 3rd, Perfect 5th, and Minor Seventh Interval above the Root Note.

- Minor 7th Arpeggios contain a Minor 3rd, Perfect 5th, and Minor Seventh Interval above the Root Note.

- Major 7th Arpeggios contain a Major 3rd, Perfect 5th, and Major Seventh Interval above the Root Note.

- Augmented 7th Arpeggios contain a Major 3rd, Augmented 5th, and Minor Seventh Interval above the Root Note.

- Half Diminished 7th Arpeggios contain a Minor 3rd, Diminished 5th, and Minor Seventh Interval above the Root Note.

- Diminished 7th Arpeggios are a set of 4 stacked Minor Third Intervals. These form a Minor 3rd, Diminished 5th, and Diminished Seventh Interval above the Root Note.

- Dominant 7th Arpeggios add a "Bluesy" quality to chord progressions. Try substituting them for Major Arpeggios.

- Minor Seventh Arpeggios can be easily substituted for Minor Arpeggios.

- Major Seventh Arpeggios add a "Jazzy" character to chord progressions. Try substituting them for Major Arpeggios.

- *Guitar Adventures 2* contains many Seventh-Chord Licks to use in Rock, Jazz, Blues, Pop, Metal, and Country.

Lesson 67: D Dominant 7th: Root Position: 6th String, 10th Fret

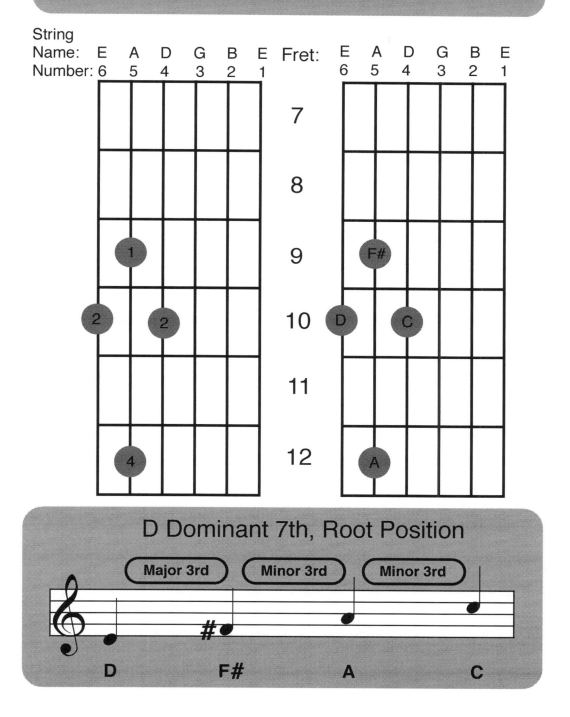

D Dominant 7th, Root Position

Lesson 68: D Dominant 7th: Root Position: 5th String, 5th Fret

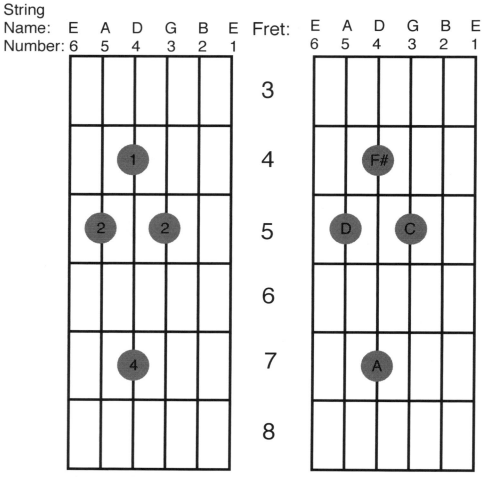

D Dominant 7th, Root Position

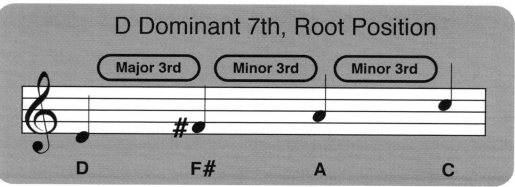

Lesson 69: D Dominant 7th: Root Position: 4th String, 12th Fret

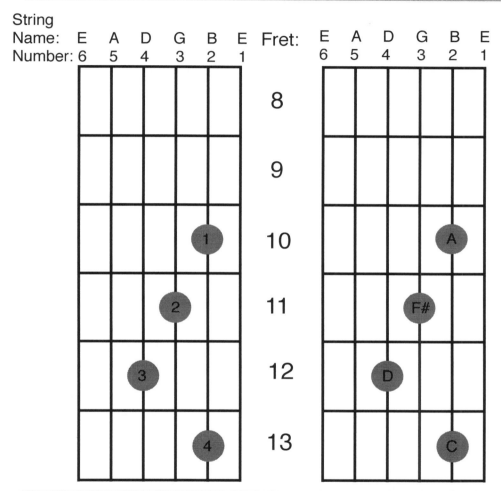

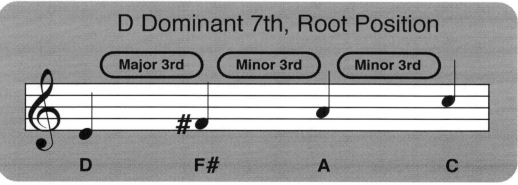

D Dominant 7th, Root Position

Lesson 70: D Dominant 7th: Root Position: 3rd String, 7th Fret

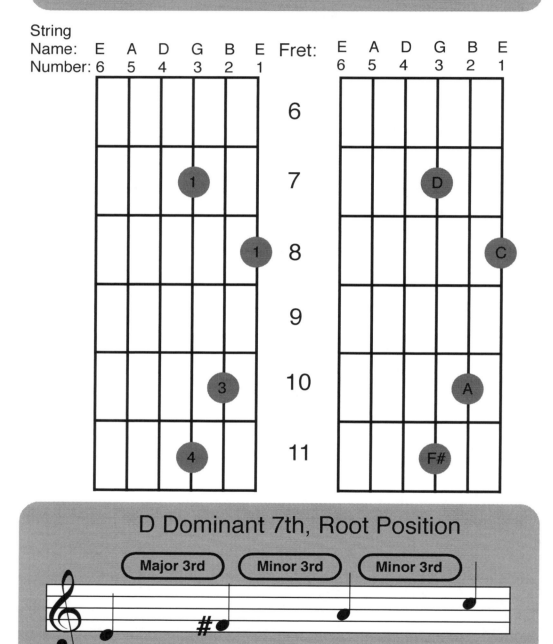

D Dominant 7th, Root Position

Lesson 71: D Dominant 7th: Root Position: 2nd String, 3rd Fret

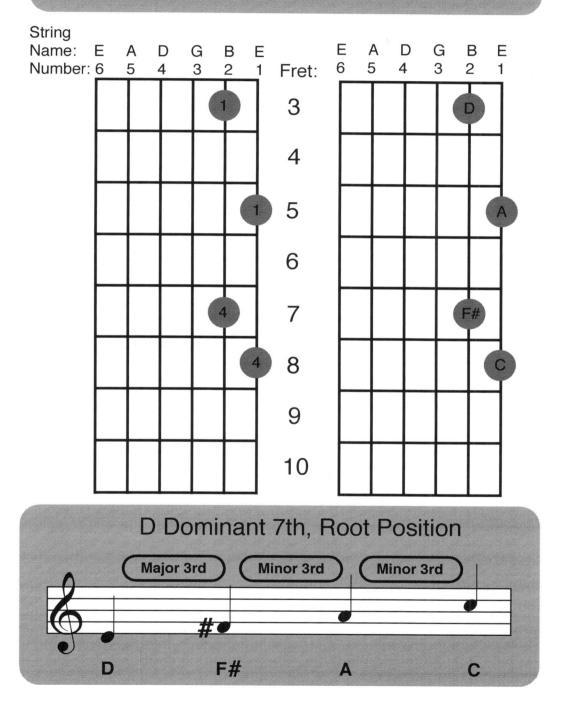

D Dominant 7th, Root Position

Lesson 72: D Minor 7th: Root Position: 6th String, 10th Fret

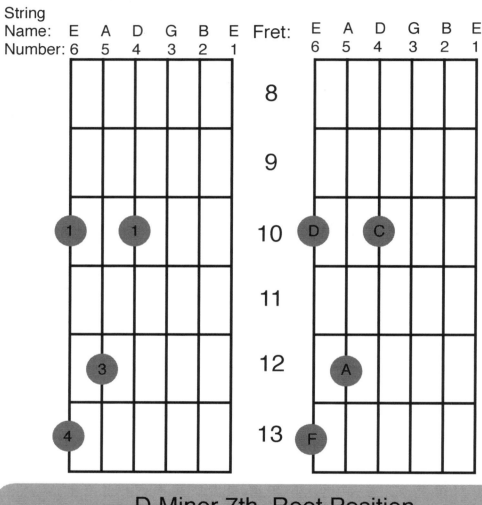

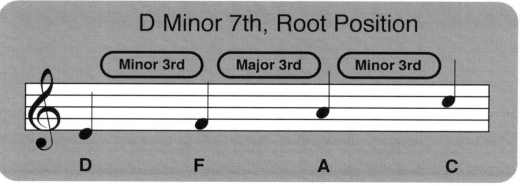

D Minor 7th, Root Position

Lesson 73: D Minor 7th: Root Position: 5th String, 5th Fret

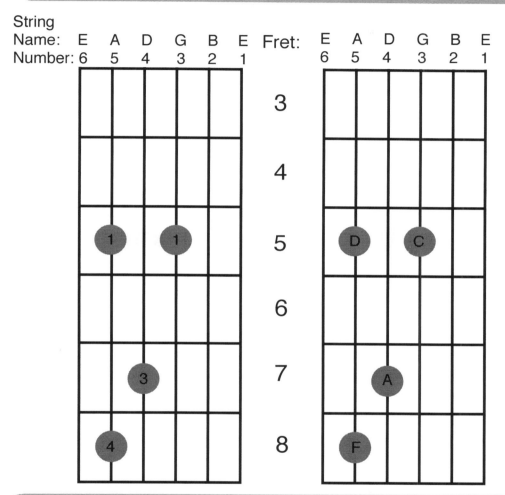

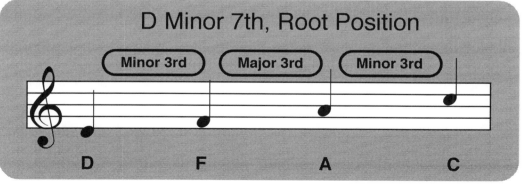

D Minor 7th, Root Position

Minor 3rd   Major 3rd   Minor 3rd

D   F   A   C

Lesson 74: D Minor 7th: Root Position: 4th String, 12th Fret

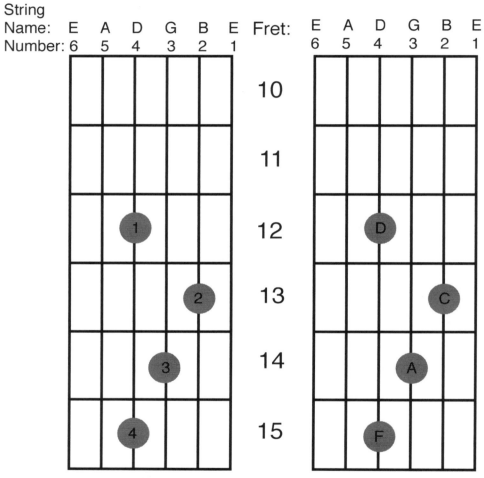

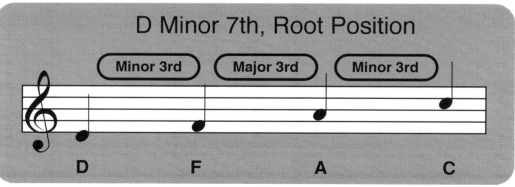

D Minor 7th, Root Position

Lesson 75: D Minor 7th: Root Position: 3rd String, 7th Fret

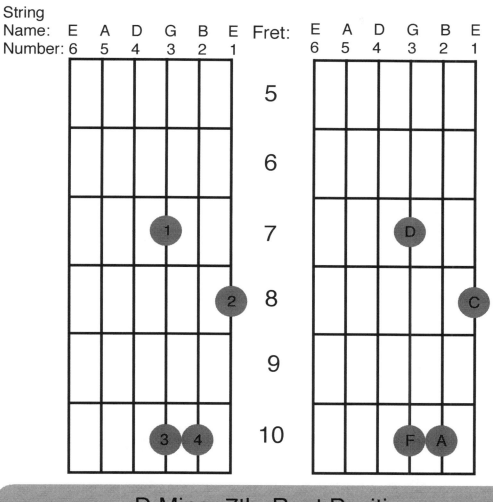

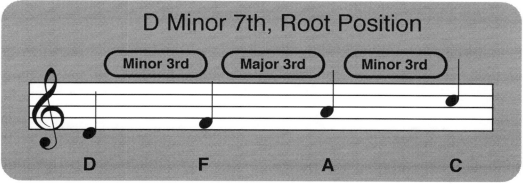

D Minor 7th, Root Position

Lesson 76: D Minor 7th: Root Position: 2nd String, 3rd Fret

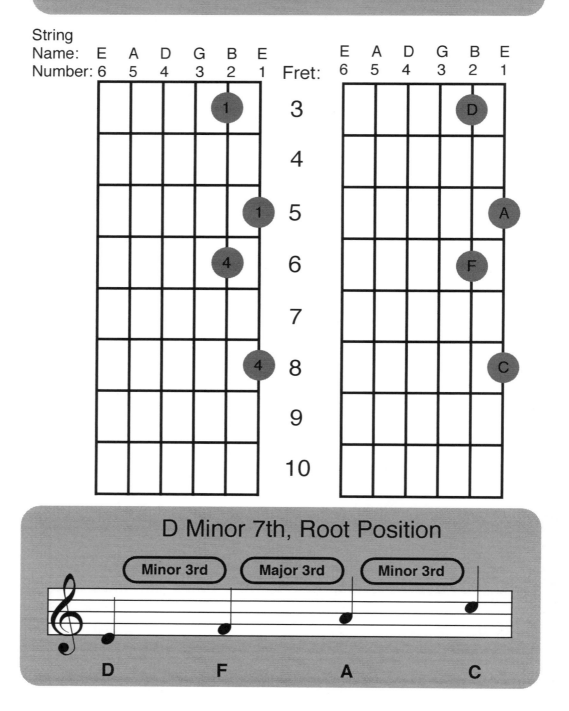

D Minor 7th, Root Position

Lesson 77: D Major 7th: Root Position: 6th String, 10th Fret

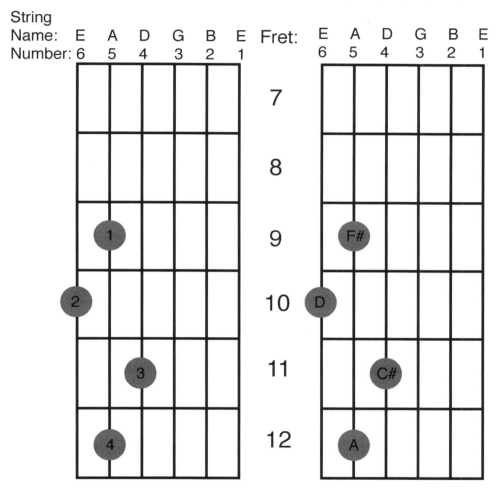

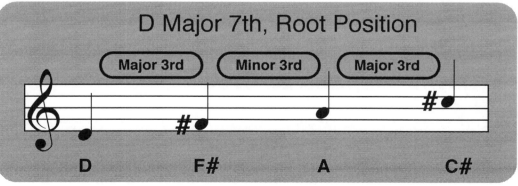

D Major 7th, Root Position

Major 3rd   Minor 3rd   Major 3rd

D   F#   A   C#

Lesson 78: D Major 7th: Root Position: 5th String, 5th Fret

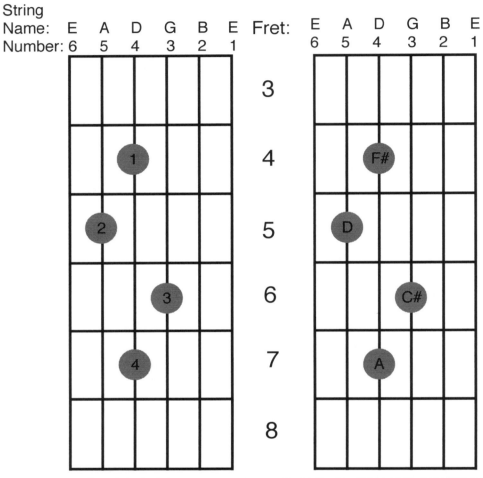

String Name: E A D G B E
Number: 6 5 4 3 2 1

Fret: 3 4 5 6 7 8

D Major 7th, Root Position

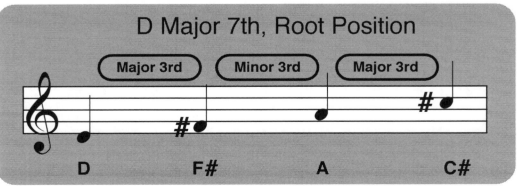

Major 3rd Minor 3rd Major 3rd

D   F#   A   C#

Lesson 79: D Major 7th: Root Position: 4th String, 12th Fret

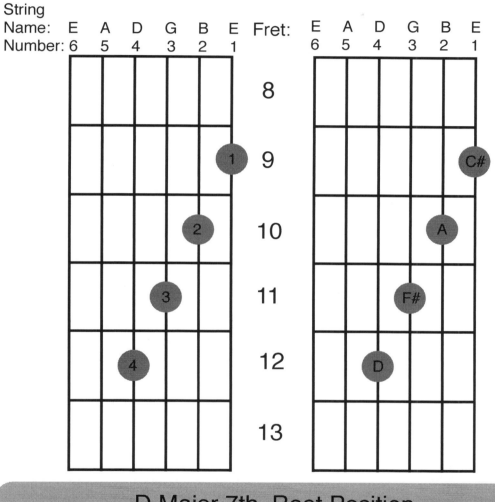

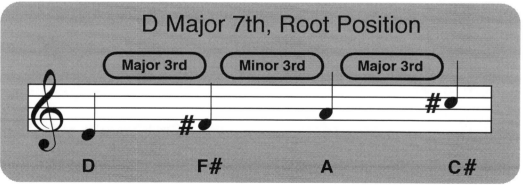

Lesson 80: D Major 7th: Root Position: 3rd String, 7th Fret

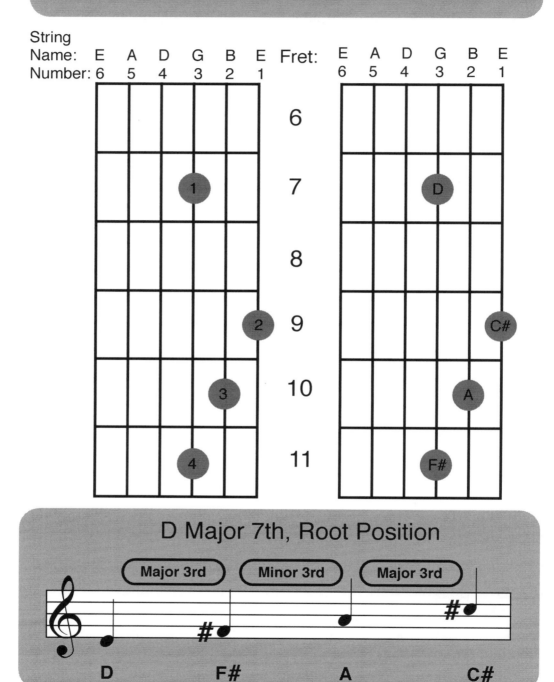

D Major 7th, Root Position

Lesson 81: D Major 7th: Root Position: 2nd String, 3rd Fret

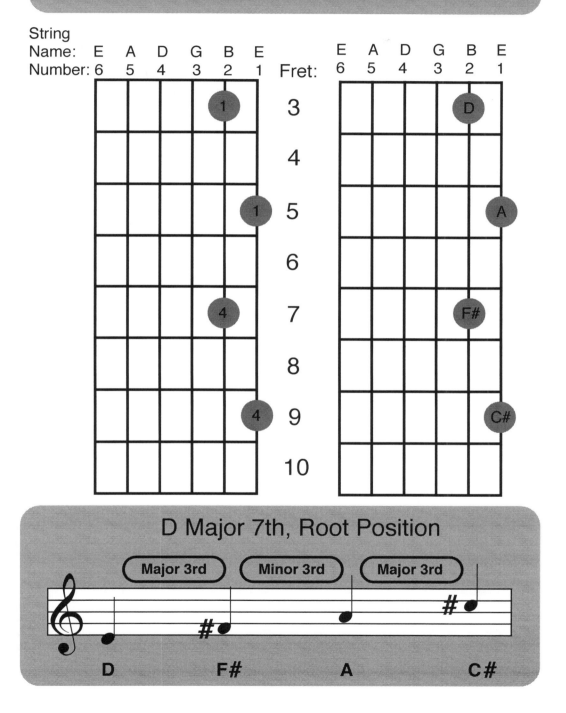

String Name: E A D G B E | E A D G B E
Number: 6 5 4 3 2 1 | Fret: | 6 5 4 3 2 1

D Major 7th, Root Position

Major 3rd | Minor 3rd | Major 3rd

D   F#   A   C#

Lesson 82: Arpeggio Substitution & Play-Along Video 5: Dominant 7th, Minor 7th & Major 7th Arpeggios

- By substituting Dominant 7th and Major 7th Arpeggios for Major Arpeggios you can greatly liven up your playing. Minor 7th Arpeggios can also be substituted for Minor Arpeggios.

- Try playing the D Dominant 7th, D Minor 7th, and D Major 7th Arpeggios over Play-Along Video 5. Listen to the difference in sound between these arpeggios. *Have Fun!*

- D7 = D Dominant 7th, Dm7 = D Minor 7th, and DM7 = D Major 7th

- Type "GuitarArpeggioHandbook" (all one word) into Youtube.

Play-Along Video 5

D7	Dm7	DM7	D7
D7	Dm7	DM7	D7
D7	Dm7	DM7	D7

Section

3

2-Octave Arpeggios

Lesson 83: D Major Triad: Root Position: 6th String, 10th Fret

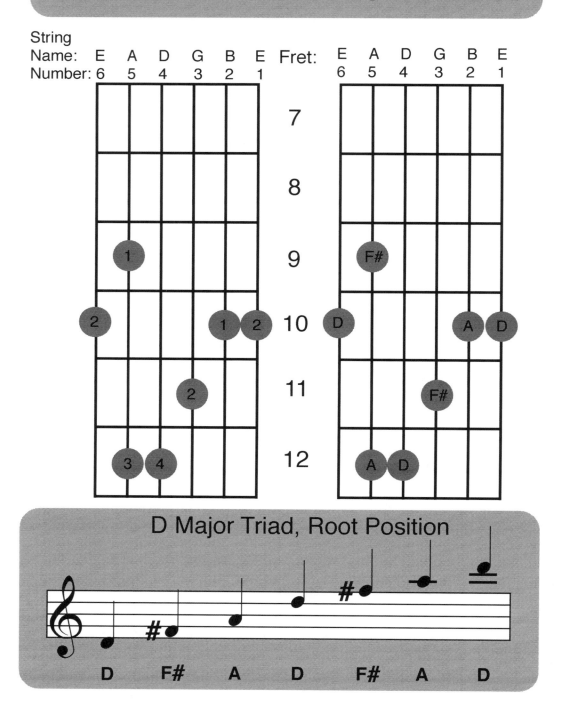

D Major Triad, Root Position

D F# A D F# A D

Lesson 84: D Major Triad: Root Position: 5th String, 5th Fret

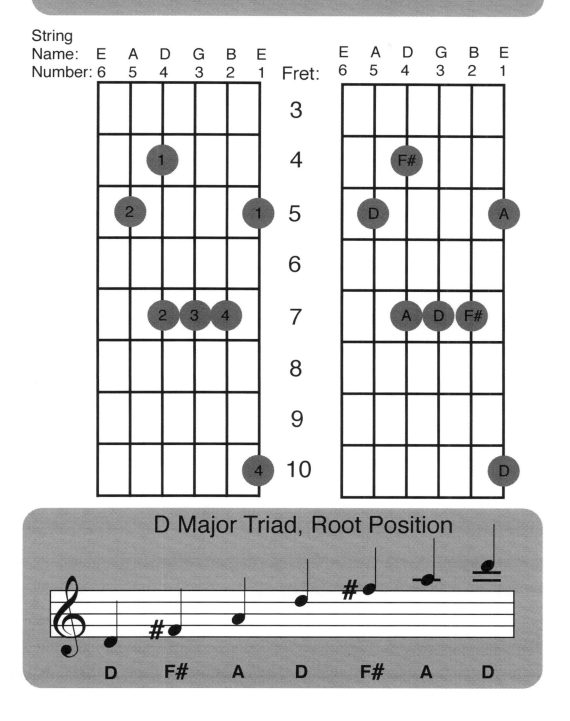

D Major Triad, Root Position

D   F#   A   D   F#   A   D

Lesson 85: D Minor Triad: Root Position: 6th String, 10th Fret

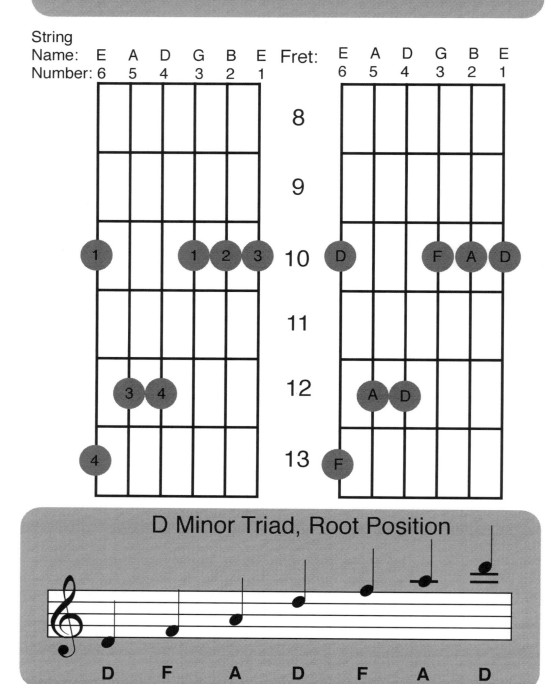

D Minor Triad, Root Position

D F A D F A D

Lesson 86: D Minor Triad: Root Position: 5th String, 5th Fret

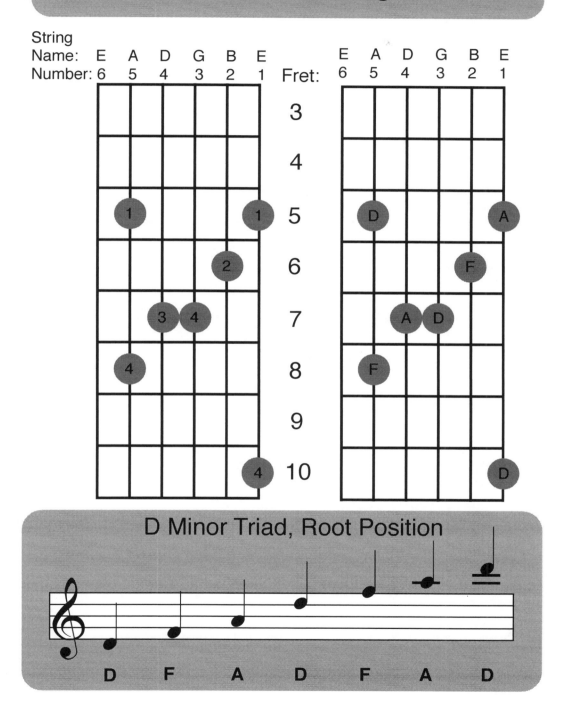

D Minor Triad, Root Position

D F A D F A D

Lesson 87: D Diminished Triad: Root Position: 6th String, 10th Fret

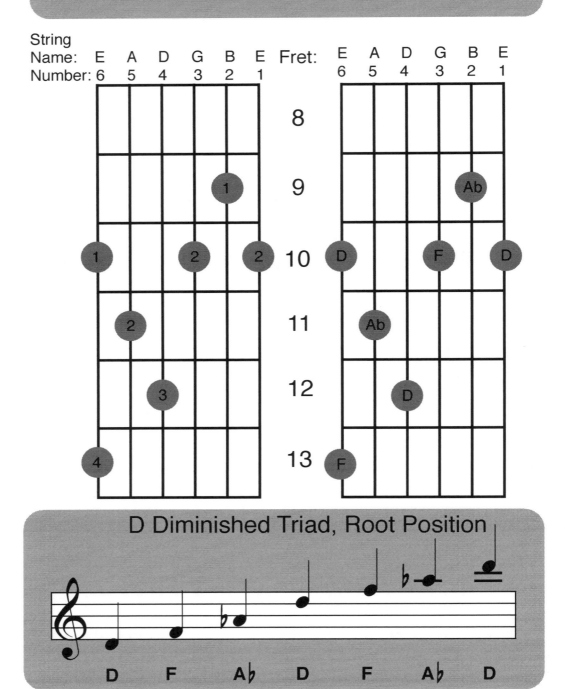

D Diminished Triad, Root Position

D   F   A♭   D   F   A♭   D

Lesson 88: D Diminished Triad: Root Position: 5th String, 5th Fret

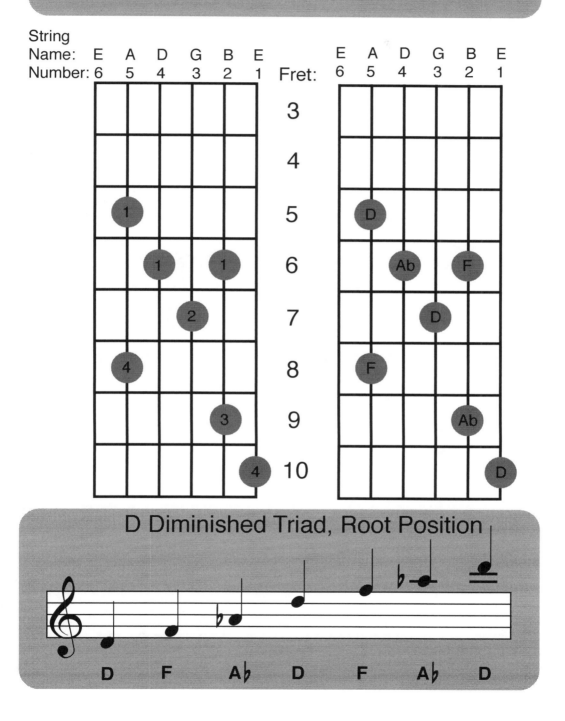

D Diminished Triad, Root Position

Lesson 89: D Augmented Triad: Root Position: 6th String, 10th Fret

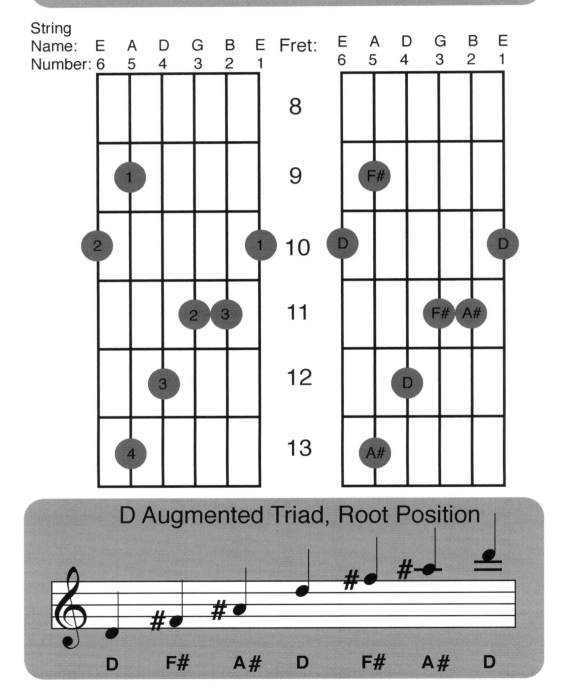

D Augmented Triad, Root Position

D   F#   A#   D   F#   A#   D

Lesson 90: D Augmented Triad: Root Position: 5th String, 5th Fret

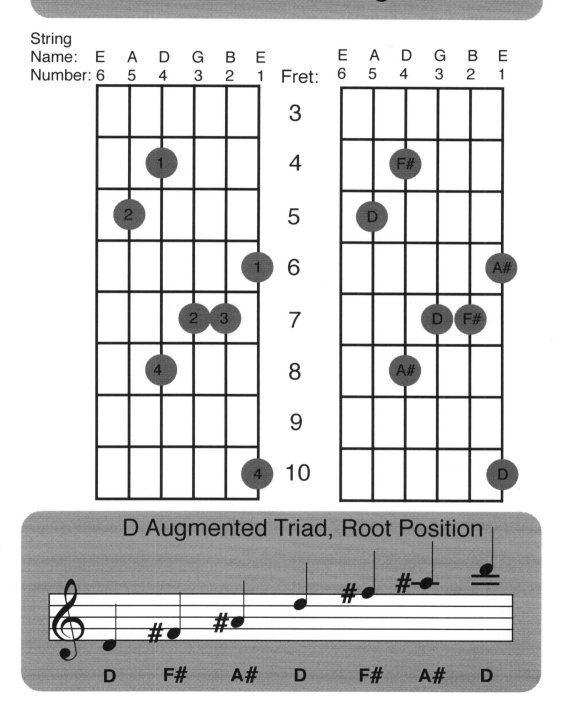

Lesson 91: Play-Along Video 6: Major, Augmented, Minor, & Diminished Arpeggios

- Try playing the D Major, D Augmented, D Minor, and D Diminished Arpeggios over Play-Along Video 6. Listen to the difference in sound among these arpeggios. **Have Fun!**

- You might also try substituting D Major 7th for D Major and D Minor 7th for D Minor.

- D Aug = D Augmented, Dm = D Minor, and D Dim = D Diminished

- Type "GuitarArpeggioHandbook" (all one word) into Youtube.

Play-Along Video 6

D	D Aug	Dm	D Dim
D	D Aug	Dm	D Dim
D	D Aug	Dm	D Dim

Lesson 92: A Major Triad: 1st Inversion: 6th String, 9th Fret

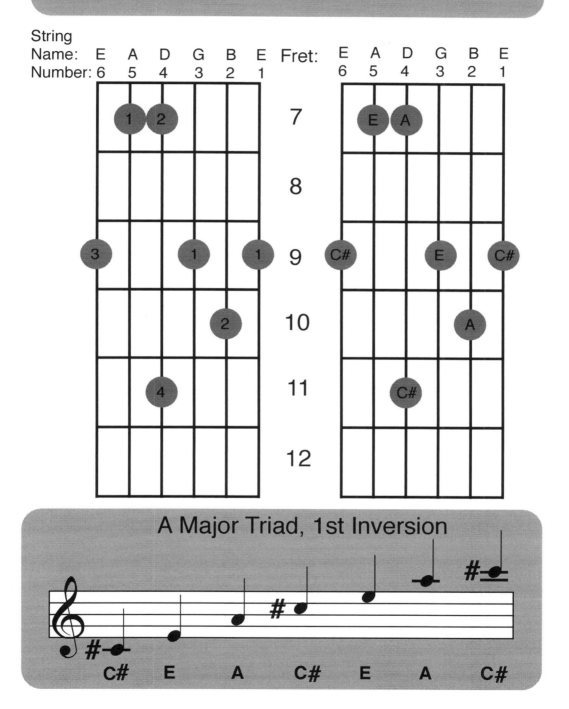

A Major Triad, 1st Inversion

Lesson 93: A Major Triad: 1st Inversion: 5th String, 4th Fret

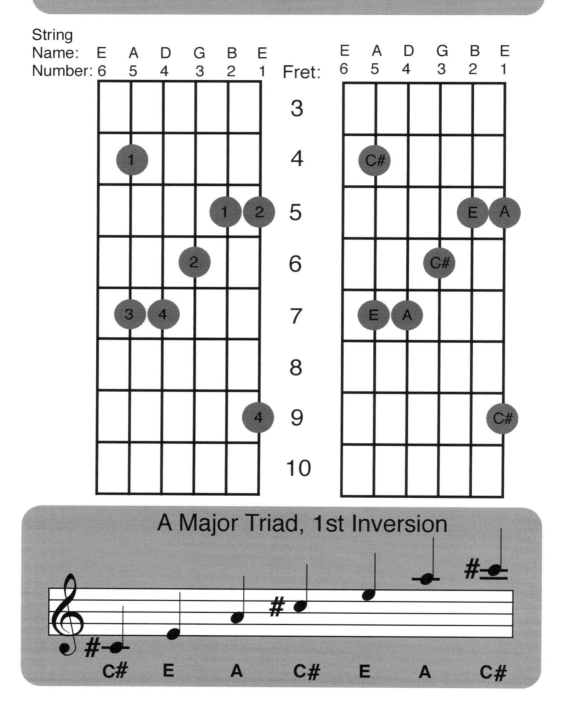

A Major Triad, 1st Inversion

Lesson 94: A Minor Triad: 1st Inversion: 6th String, 8th Fret

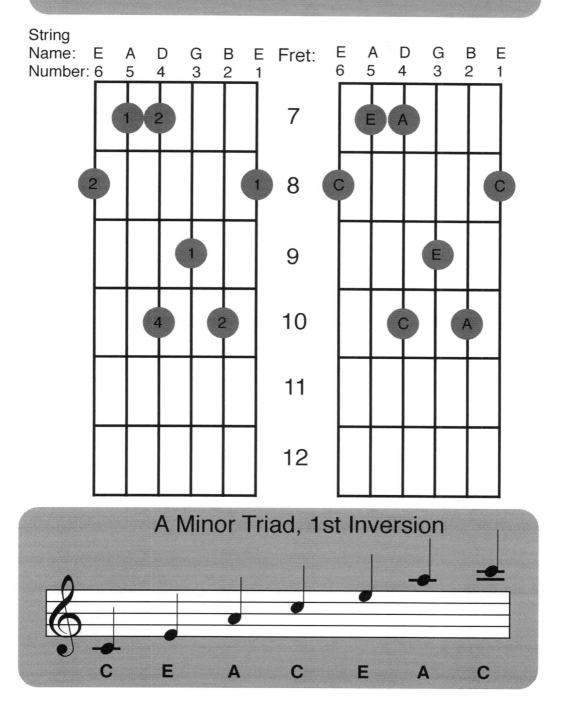

A Minor Triad, 1st Inversion

C   E   A   C   E   A   C

Lesson 95: A Minor Triad: 1st Inversion: 5th String, 3rd Fret

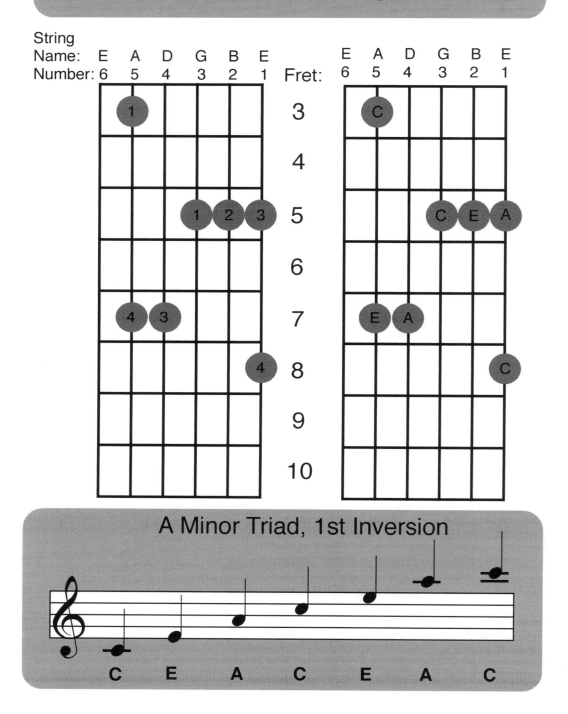

A Minor Triad, 1st Inversion

Lesson 96: D Dominant 7th: Root Position: 6th String, 10th Fret

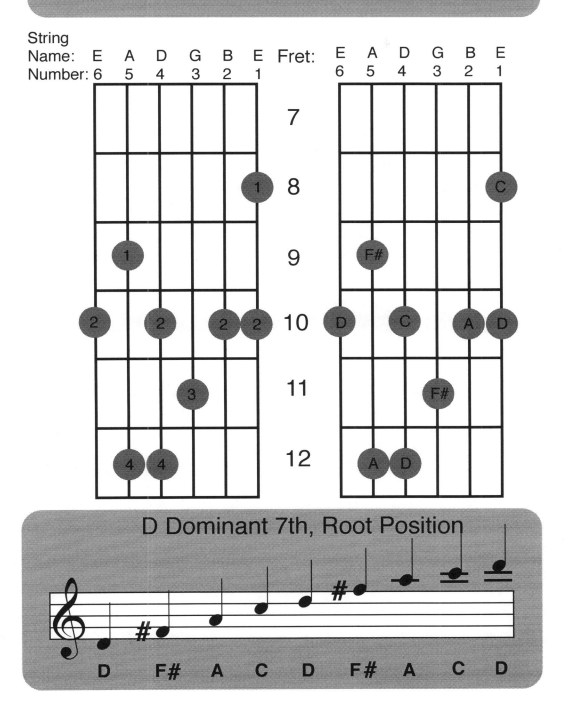

D Dominant 7th, Root Position

Lesson 97: D Dominant 7th: Root Position: 5th String, 5th Fret

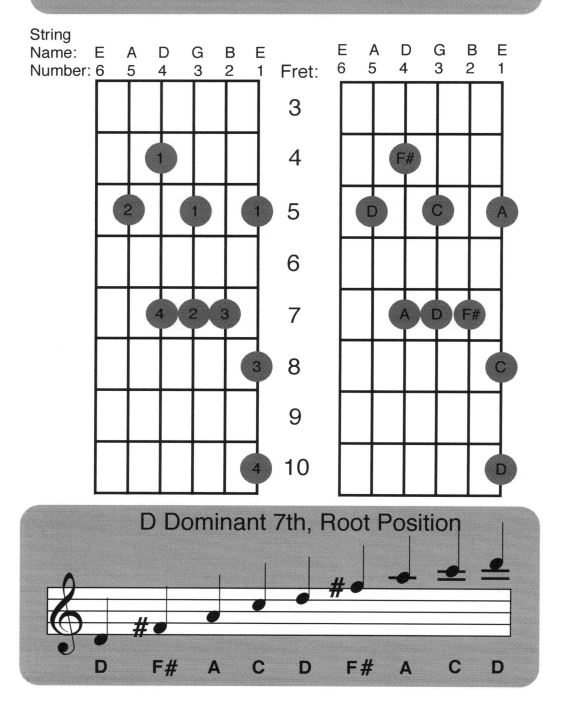

D Dominant 7th, Root Position

Lesson 98: D Minor 7th: Root Position: 6th String, 10th Fret

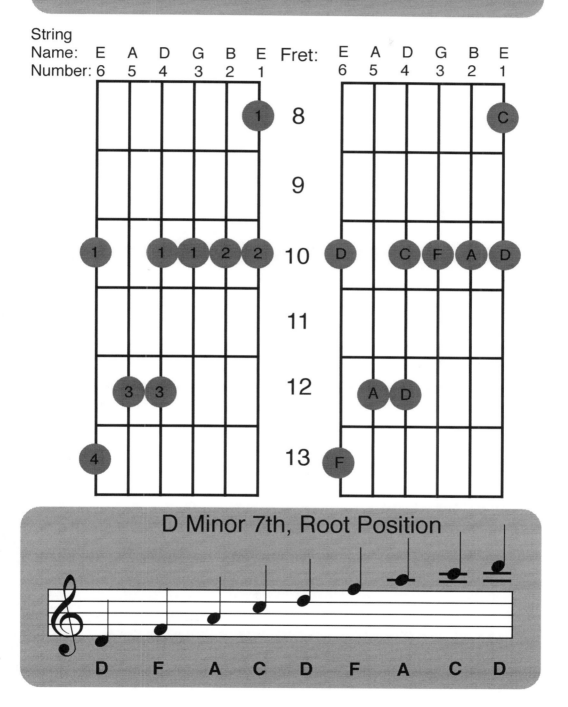

D Minor 7th, Root Position

Lesson 99: D Minor 7th: Root Position: 5th String, 5th Fret

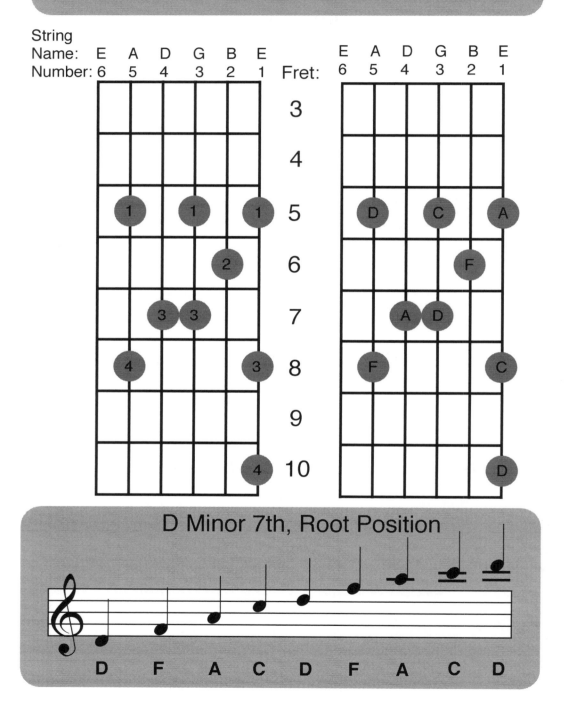

D Minor 7th, Root Position

D F A C D F A C D

Lesson 100: D Major 7th: Root Position: 6th String, 10th Fret

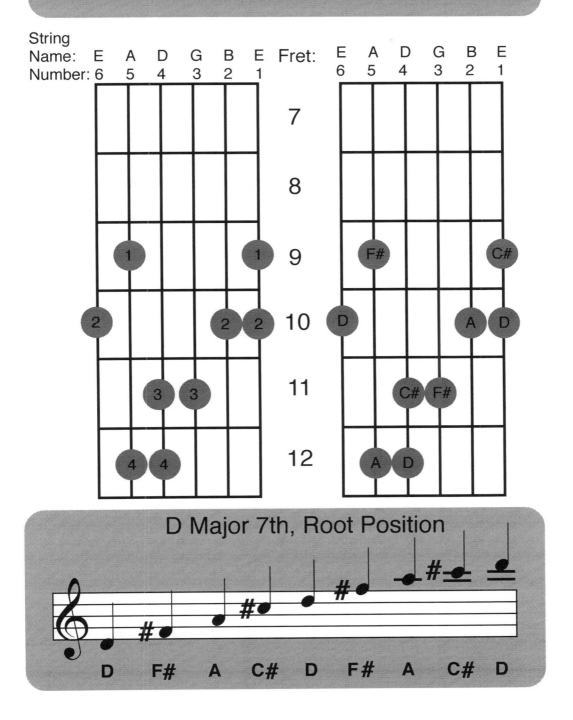

D Major 7th, Root Position

D   F#   A   C#   D   F#   A   C#   D

Lesson 101: D Major 7th: Root Position: 5th String, 5th Fret

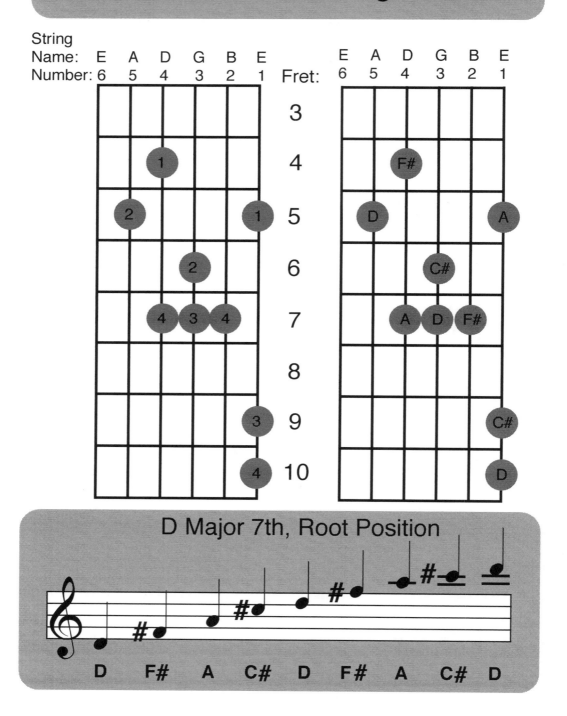

D Major 7th, Root Position

D   F#   A   C#   D   F#   A   C#   D

Lesson 102: D Diminished 7th: Root Position: 6th String, 10th Fret

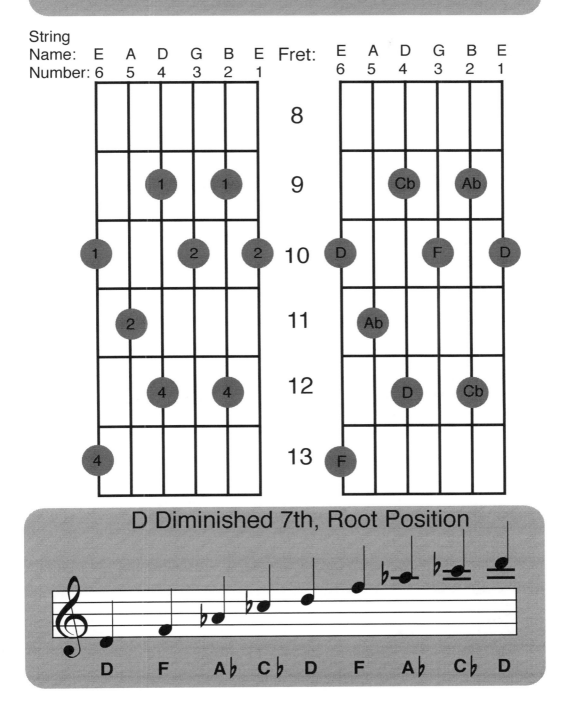

D Diminished 7th, Root Position

Lesson 103: D Diminished 7th: Root Position: 5th String, 5th Fret

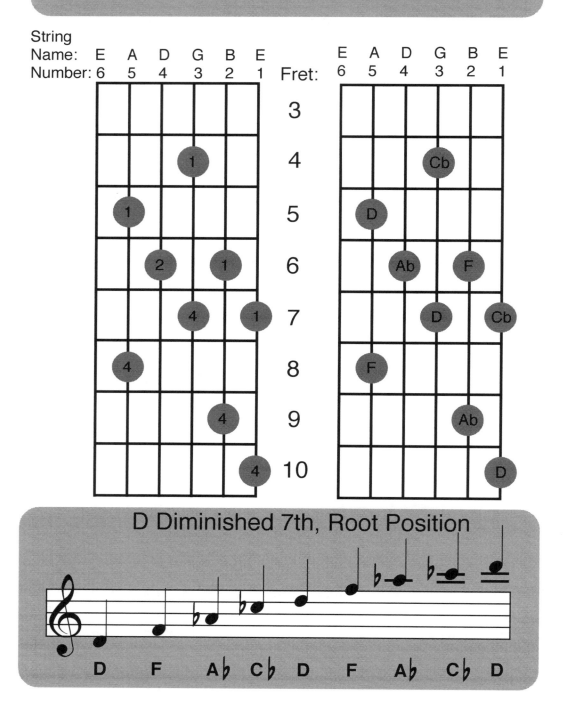

D Diminished 7th, Root Position

Lesson 104: D Augmented 7th: Root Position: 6th String, 10th Fret

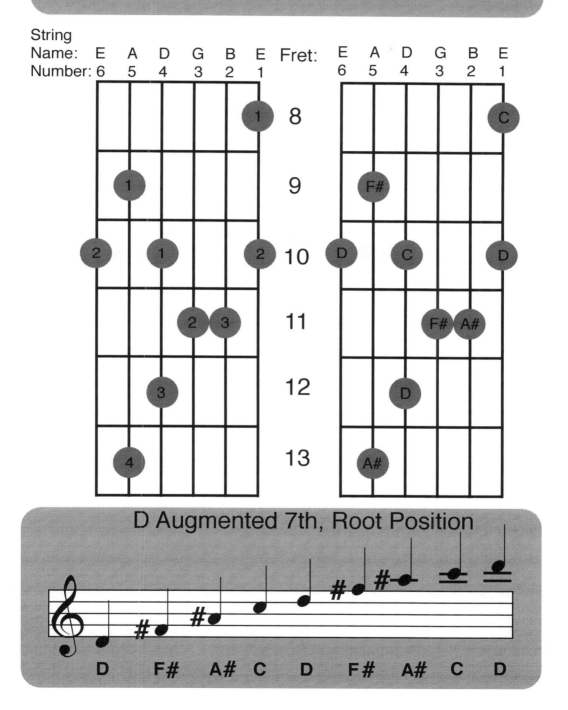

D Augmented 7th, Root Position

Lesson 105: D Half-Diminished 7th: Root Position: 6th String, 10th Fret

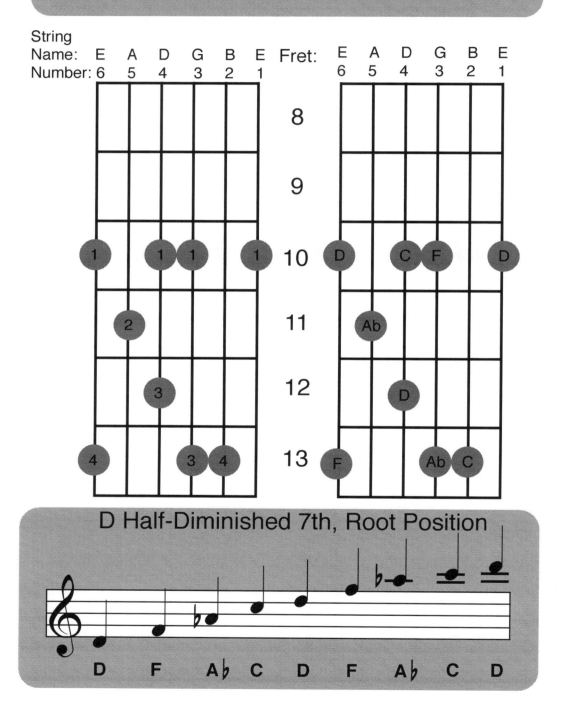

D Half-Diminished 7th, Root Position

Lesson 106: D Major 6th:
Root Position: 6th String, 10th Fret

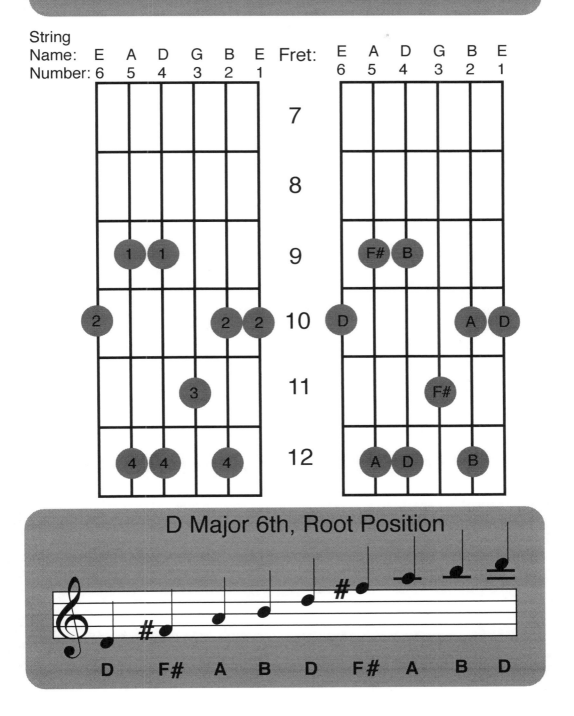

D Major 6th, Root Position

D F# A B D F# A B D

Lesson 107: Play-Along Video 7: Rockabilly in G Major

- This Play-Along Video is a high-energy Rockabilly track. It follows a standard 12-Bar Blues (I, IV, V) progression in G Major.
- Try playing your Dominant 7th Arpeggios over the chord changes.
- Also, try substituting your 9th, 11th, and 13th Arpeggios for the Dominant 7th Arpeggios. For example, play a C Dominant 9th Arpeggio instead of a C Dominant 7th Arpeggio or play a D 13th Arpeggio instead of a D Dominant 7th Arpeggio.
- Type "GuitarArpeggioHandbook" (all one word) into Youtube.
- *Have Fun!*

Play-Along Video 7

G7	G7	G7	G7
C7	C7	G7	G7
D7	C7	G7	G7

Lesson 108: D Minor 6th: Root Position: 6th String, 10th Fret

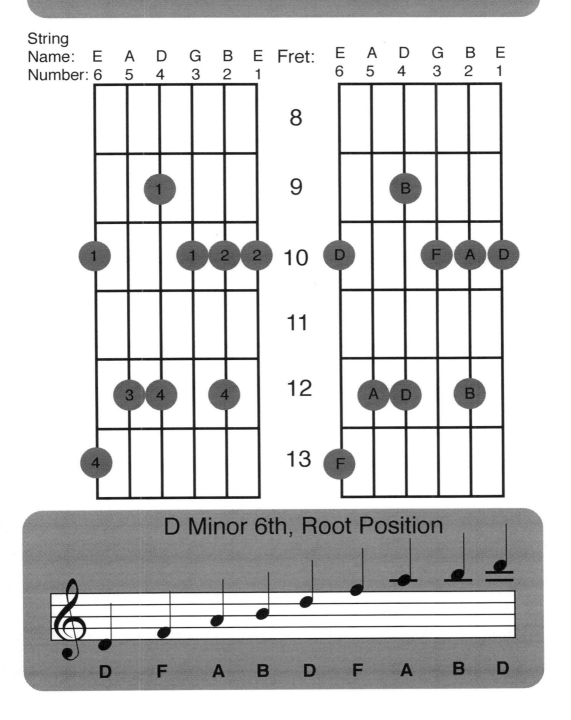

D Minor 6th, Root Position

Lesson 109: D Dominant 9th: Root Position: 6th String, 10th Fret

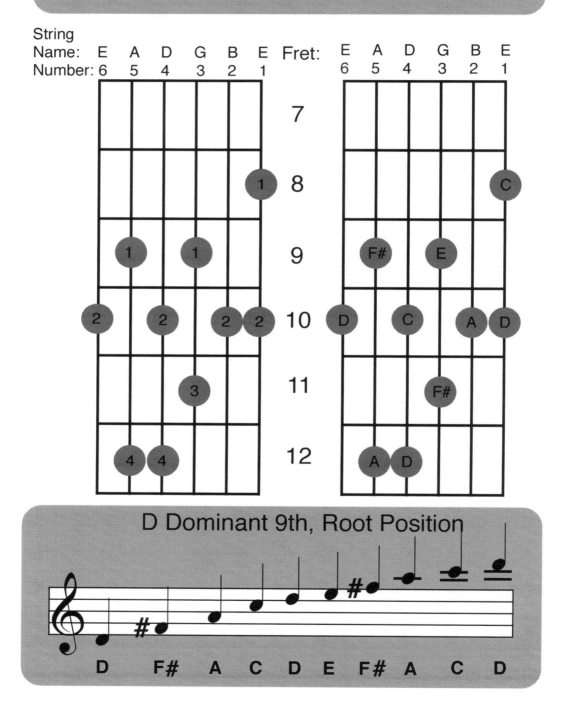

D Dominant 9th, Root Position

D   F#   A   C   D   E   F#   A   C   D

Lesson 110: D Minor 9th: Root Position: 6th String, 10th Fret

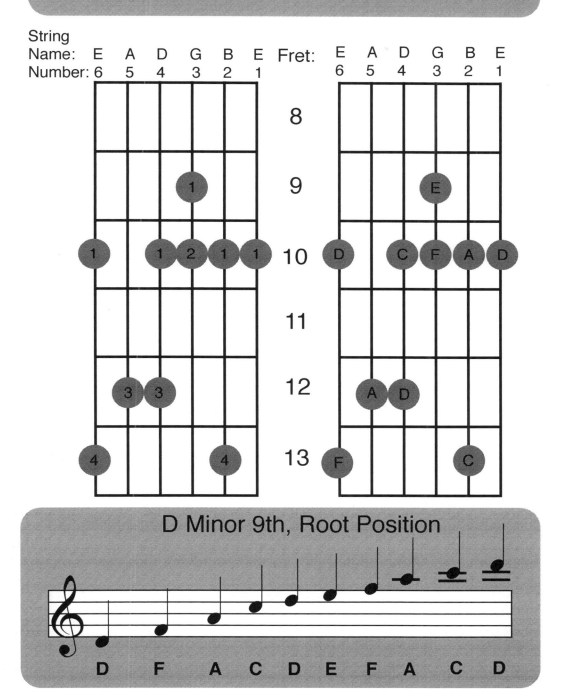

D Minor 9th, Root Position

Lesson 111: D Dominant 11th: Root Position: 6th String, 10th Fret

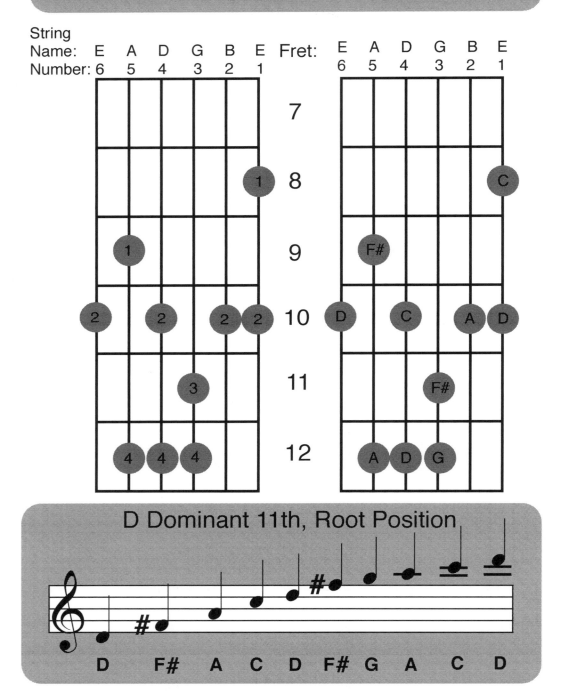

D Dominant 11th, Root Position

Lesson 112: D Dominant 13th: Root Position: 6th String, 10th Fret

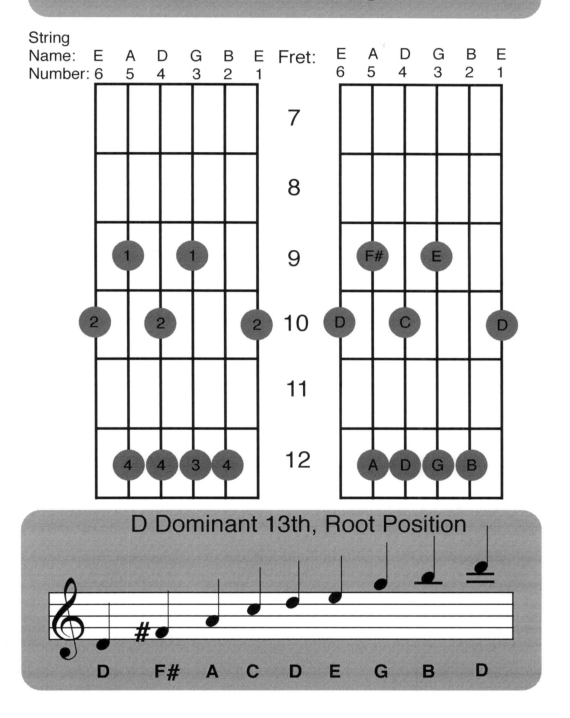

D Dominant 13th, Root Position

D F# A C D E G B D

A Major Triad, 3 Octaves, Root Position

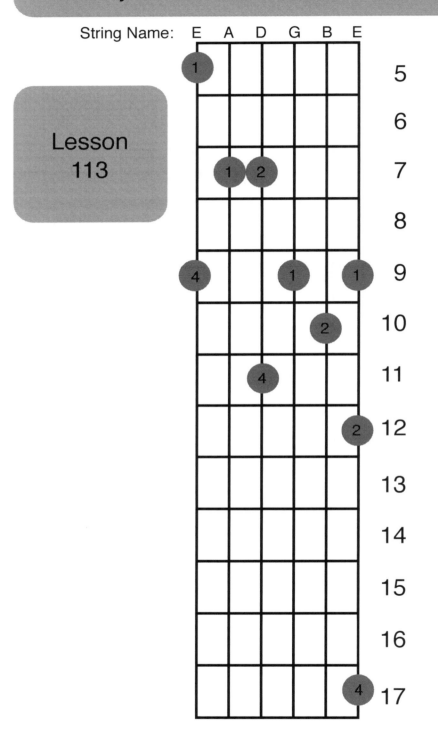

A Minor Triad, 3 Octaves, Root Position

Lesson 114

Congratulations! You have made it to the finish line. You now have added some powerful tools to your guitar playing and songwriting. I hope that this book has opened your ears to some new sounds and helped you grow as an artist. Good luck! DF

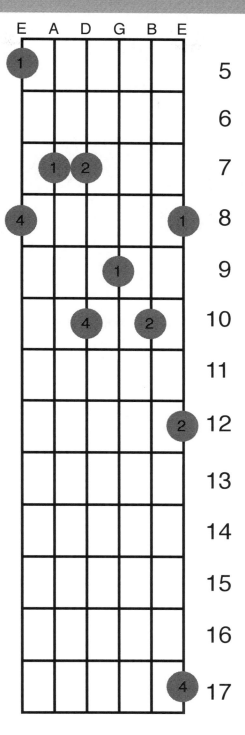

String Name: E A D G B E

5
6
7
8
9
10
11
12
13
14
15
16
17

Damon Ferrante is a composer, guitarist, and music writer. When he was 8 years old, his uncle left an old electric guitar, which was in two pieces (neck and body separated) at his parents' house. Damon put the guitar together using some old screws and duct tape. That was the beginning of a wild ride through Rock, Jazz, Classical Music, and Opera that has spanned over 20 years. Along the way, Ferrante has had performances at Carnegie Hall, Symphony Space, and throughout the US and Europe. He has taught on the music faculties of Seton Hall University and Montclair State University. He is the director of Steeplechase Arts & Productions, a company that he founded in 2003. Damon lives in New York City and Milan, Italy.

His other guitar books are available online and in retail bookstores. If you like this book, you might want to check out *Guitar Adventures, Beginner Rock Guitar Lessons, and Piano Scales, Chords, Arpeggios Lessons.*

Check Out Steeplechasemusic.com for Free Lessons Videos Licks and Interviews!

Dedication

This book is dedicated to the hundreds of students I have had the honor to work with at Montclair State University and Seton Hall University. I am grateful to them all for the grace that they showed me as students and artists. Here is a short list: Nicole DeMaio, Andrew Digrius, Liz Epstein, Harry Hipwell, Annelise McGuire, John McLean, Erica Moyer, Domenick Panfile, Chris Pizzute, Stefanie Santoro, Leah Stark, Steve Tortora, Ben Whitford, Laura Baker, Chuck Comanda, Andrew Ludewig, Christina McCall, Billy Merrill, Matt Olsson, Arielle Perrusio, Bryan Stepneski, Jamie Gebhardt, Ryan McCausland, Miguel Morales, Laura Nunez, Chelsey Ristaino, Angelina Hamada, Stefon Gaines, Rosario Toscano, John Carega, Catherine Tsang, Evan Ruggiero, Carli Barolin, Ken Hanasaka, Alejandro Moumdjian, Kathryn Pfuhler, Steve Mancine, Lauren Arencibia, Kristina Nieskens, Jeff Cash, Lauren Cerra, Bruno Gasulla, Natalie Hernandez, Paul Lasko, Miguel Mercado, Sam Petrone, Ian Witt, Mark Badaczewski, Josephine Bhola, and Mark Bitar

43103876R00156

Made in the USA
Middletown, DE
30 April 2017